FAITH AND A LIFE JACKET

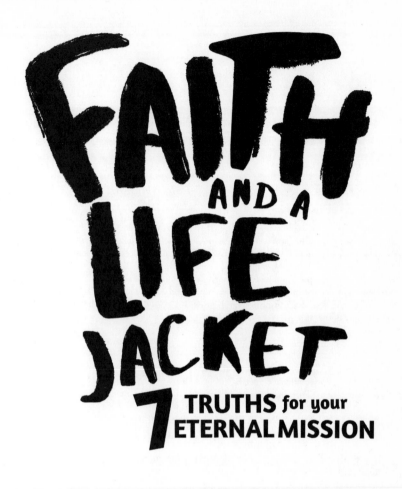

FAITH AND A LIFE JACKET

7 TRUTHS for your ETERNAL MISSION

BEN BERNARDS

CFI
An imprint of Cedar Fort, Inc.
Springville, Utah

ISBN 13: 978-1-4621-1904-2

Published by CFI, an imprint of Cedar Fort, Inc.
2373 W. 700 S., Springville, UT 84663
Distributed by Cedar Fort, Inc., www.cedarfort.com

LIBRARY OF CONGRESS CATALOGING-IN-PUBLICATION DATA

Names: Bernards, Ben, 1978- author.
Title: Faith and a life jacket : 7 truths for your eternal mission / Ben
  Bernards.
Description: Springville, Utah : CFI, an imprint of Cedar Fort, Inc., [2016]
  | Includes bibliographical references and index.
Identifiers: LCCN 2016022612 (print) | LCCN 2016023844 (ebook) | ISBN
  9781462119042 (perfect bound : alk. paper) | ISBN 9781462126835 (epub,
  pdf, and mobi)
Subjects: LCSH: Christian life--Mormon authors. | Mormon missionaries.
Classification: LCC BX8656 .B474 2016 (print) | LCC BX8656 (ebook) | DDC
  248.4/88332--dc23
LC record available at https://lccn.loc.gov/2016022612

Cover design by Kinsey Beckett
Cover design © 2016 by Cedar Fort, Inc.
Edited and typeset by Deborah Spencer

Printed in the United States of America

10 9 8 7 6 5 4 3 2 1

Printed on acid-free paper

To my dad, the first missionary I ever knew.

CONTENTS

FOREWORD

I first met Ben when he presented at an EFY session I directed. The youth loved him! His classes were packed and listeners were mesmerized. They ate up his stories of serving his mission on remote islands in the Pacific. I loved that he was teaching important principles that would bless the lives of these future missionaries no matter where they might serve. That's a delicate balance to keep and Ben has now pulled off the same amazing feat in this book.

You will love Ben's down-to-earth writing style. You will feel like you are engaging in a conversation with him rather than reading a book. Ben speaks and writes with honesty about the challenges faced by missionaries, but he is quick to share solutions. Scriptures come to life as he links them with personal experiences.

You'll read of missionaries meeting with great chiefs and exciting conversion stories, but you'll also read how Ben dealt with rejection from investigators and a painful "Dear John" letter from his girlfriend back home. You'll see how he encountered people living in extreme poverty and learned to love those people with his whole heart.

Some of his advice is practical: Keep a journal, keep your apartment clean, and make time count. Other advice will take you many years to fully implement: Be teachable, be grateful, and let go of the little stuff. All the advice will put you on the road to becoming a great missionary and a great person.

I would love to make Ben's chapter on measuring success required reading for everyone. Too many feel like failures because we allow others to impose unrealistic goals and expectations on us. Ben reminds readers that success can be measured in multiple ways and that we all need to see our efforts through God's eyes.

I hope you remember what you read in Ben's book, but years from now you may or may not remember all the details about the seven hard lessons Ben has learned and shared. What you need to remember for sure is that God will teach you just as He taught Ben. Don't let anything stop you from serving your mission! You'll discover, as Ben did, that you never serve alone. God will help and strengthen you. When you stand with Christ, the hard lessons always become easy. "Take my yoke upon you," the Savior said. "For my yoke is easy" (Matthew 11: 29–30).

–Brad Wilcox

INTRODUCTION

'll never forget the day I opened my mission call. The large, rectangular envelope had been lying on our kitchen table all day, awaiting members of my large Utah family to come home from work and school. I was so excited to finally learn where I'd be spending the next two years of my life! When everyone had finally gathered, the cameras were rolling, and the friendly bets had been placed, I tore open the envelope and saw the words that I'd been dreaming of for months: *"Dear Elder Bernards, you have been called to serve as a representative of the Church of Jesus Christ of Latter-day Saints."* Before I pulled out the rest of the letter, I peeked inside and quickly scanned down the page to try to find the best part—the assignment location. My eyes locked on to the words "Fiji Islands" and a massive grin spread over my face while my parents hollered at me to pull the rest out and read it. I did, my sisters screamed, my brothers *oohed* and *ahhed*, and we danced around like we thought Fijians would. Then of course I ran off to grab an encyclopedia to figure out just where the heck Fiji was. (Google Maps wasn't around just yet.)

So began The Long Wait—that agonizingly slow time between opening the call and actually reporting to the MTC, when it feels like everything goes wrong and struggles are mysteriously magnified. Six excruciating months after getting my call, I finally touched down in the islands of the South Pacific—only to realize that despite all my efforts, I still didn't feel ready for real life.

Now this isn't to say that my preparations were in vain or that the Missionary Training Center wasn't helpful. It had accomplished its purpose: to train me. But once the training was complete, the simulations were over, and I was thrown out into the reality of missionary work, I instantly felt like I was out of my league and in way too deep. What I thought would be a simple, straightforward life instead turned out to be a crucible of constant trials, close-calls, heart-wrenching struggles, soul-crushing disappointments, and straight-up miracles—each one reminding me that despite all the books I'd read, talks I'd listened to, classes I'd attended, money I'd spent, and supplies I'd gathered, there was still so much about the gospel and life that I had yet to learn.

THE SEVEN TRUTHS

Someone once said, "Experience is a hard teacher—she gives the test first and the lessons afterward." Sometimes the "tests" came with easy, obvious life lessons that I was able to learn right away, while other times it felt like I was taking the same test over and over again! Eventually I started to see a pattern emerging—nearly every test and lesson shared one or more aspects of a core set of interlocked Truths. They appeared repeatedly, guiding my efforts to serve like lighthouses gleaming through the darkness of a cyclone. As I came to understand these Truths and how they interacted with each other, I realized that not only would they help me through the difficulty of missionary life, but they would anchor me through *any* trial I would face, at *any* point in my life to come. I call them "The Seven Truths for Your Eternal Mission."

Truth 1: It's Going to Be Harder than You Think, but It's Possible with God's Help

Truth 2: Evil Is Real, but God Is More Powerful

Truth 3: Miracles Happen, and They're Unlocked by Patient Obedience

Truth 4: Timing Is Everything, and It's in God's Hands

Truth 5: Love the People. There Is No Substitute

Truth 6: Success Ain't What You Think; God Measures It Differently

Truth 7: Forget Yourself and Go to Work

Since my return from the mission field, I've spoken with hundreds of youths, pre-missionaries, and returned missionaries, and listened to how they too have discovered these same Truths, even across multiple cultures and languages. I quickly discovered that these principles are primal, universal, and have been learned and applied by countless missionaries the world over. In many ways they are self-evident and need little explanation. But while they may be common *knowledge*, they are not always common *practice*. Some missionaries might only discover one or two of them during their whole mission, while others may return from service having never learned a thing. (What a tragedy!) But don't worry—wherever you are in your missionary journey, you'll find these principles can be discovered, internalized, and applied to *any* stage of your life, even as an RM, college student, or young adult. Because these Truths aren't just for missionaries; they're for everyone. Heck, if you're anything like me, you'll probably need several tests before you really *get it*.

BRIDGING THE GAP

The Church has published a workbook for pre-missionaries titled "Adjusting to Missionary Life." It describes the four major stages every missionary goes through facing new situations:

1) **Anticipation**—you feel eager for the challenge and have an increased sense of purpose and greater dedication to your God.
2) **Discovering the Unexpected**—when faced with the difficult realities of missionary life, you start to miss your home, family, and friends. Self-doubts arise and you may doubt your decision to serve. Homesickness, stress, and anxiety are quite common at this stage.
3) **"I Can Do This"**—you become better adjusted to the demands of missionary life, your teaching and language skills begin to improve, and you resolve the tensions you've been facing.
4) **Emotional Self-Reliance**—you feel comfortable navigating the daily routine, you recognize your own strengths and abilities, you feel confident about your skills and have integrated well with the team around you. (see "Adjusting to Missionary Life," p. 52)

As you progress through the four stages, your confidence in

your abilities will grow and increase. You will gain new skills, learn how to handle each challenge with cheerfulness and faith, and you'll achieve higher levels of self-reliance and maturity. It's natural to expect your progress and growth to be linear and straightforward.

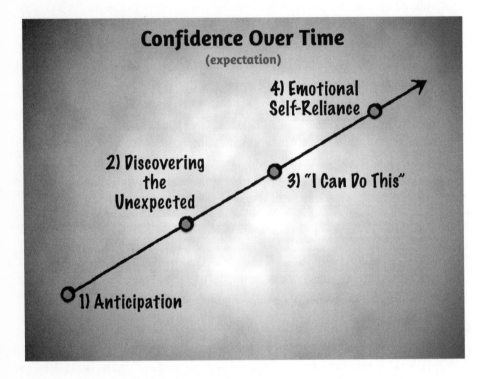

But reality is rarely that simple.

When the Unexpected hit me hard, my self-confidence started to plummet and I realized I was facing a *huge* Ability Gap between Stages 2 and 3. The breadth of the Ability Gap (and the Gulf of Self-Doubt below it) will vary from person to person, but it is inescapable—it is a reflection of the reality that our challenges are, well, *challenging*. God will never ask us to do the truly impossible, but neither will He ask us to do merely that which is comfortable.

Sooner or later, the fires of Anticipation will dim, the thrill of the Unexpected and New will fade. Discouragement and doubt will entice you to give up and walk away from it all. That's when you'll face the Decision Point—the moment where you get to choose how you will respond to your challenges: rising up to them and pressing forward with faith, or remaining disengaged and frustrated.

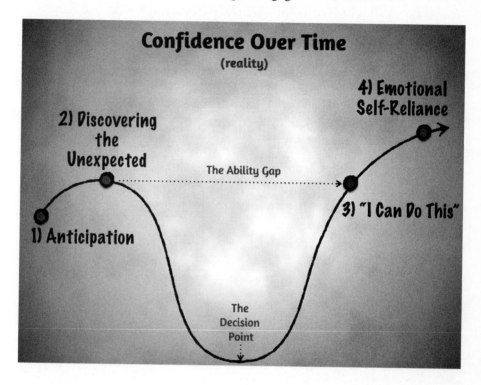

This book is designed to help you press **forward** and **upward**. If you find yourself right at the cusp of "Discovering the Unexpected," this book will help you construct a faith scaffolding and cross to the "I Can Do This" stage. If you have already sunk into your own Gulf of Self-Doubt, the principles herein will help you climb your way out, growing in confidence and ability as you inch your way up and out, to true Emotional Self-Reliance. And no matter where you are on your missionary journey, these Truths will reinforce your faith in God, your ability to communicate with Him, and your own growing ministerial capabilities.

Where the MTC lays a foundation for success, these Seven Truths will build the next level of ability and skill needed to serve in God's vineyard. Consider them the source code for effective missionary work.

If you're reading this book, you're probably thinking of serving a mission or you may know someone who is. You probably want to not just be *prepared* to serve, but be prepared *well*. So whether you're serving in your home country, stateside, or foreign-speaking or whether you're a greenie, a trainer, or the senior AP, knowing and applying the Seven Truths will bring clarity and perspective to your mission and enable deeper, more meaningful growth of your testimony and the testimonies of those you teach.

Ezra Taft Benson once said, "Some are better prepared to serve the Lord the first month in the mission field than some who are returning home after twenty-four months. We want young men entering the mission field 'on the run.'"[1] This book is designed to get you up to speed *fast*. Few things have brought me greater joy than to hear how these Truths have blessed someone's life as they've embarked to serve their fellow men—let's get to work!

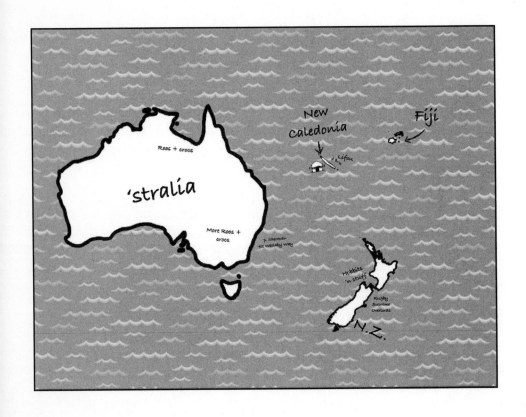

TRUTH #1

It's Going to Be Harder than You Think, but It's Possible with God's Help

> "Hardships often prepare ordinary people
> for an extraordinary destiny."
>
> —*C. S. Lewis, Mere Christianity*

So this is what it feels like, I thought to myself, sitting on the floor of our little grass hut in the jungle.

My panicked, terrified mind was starting to go numb as I realized I had no escape from the angry tribal natives that were planning to attack my companion and me that night.

So this is what it feels like when someone asks you, "Are you ready to die for what you believe?"

I'd only been on my mission a few months, and everything I thought I knew about life as a missionary had been completely thrown out the window . . . er . . . hut door.

A WARNING

The LDS congregation on the tropical island of Lifou was very small: our branch was comprised of just a single family, the Alikis, a few of their cousins, and two of their tribal neighbors. Papa Aliki was the head of the clan and our branch president. He had opened his home to the missionaries and given us a place in one of their huts in the jungle. Life was simple and sublime in the jungle—we'd cook over an open fire, use our hunting dogs and machetes to run down wild game in the jungle, pull fish from the ocean, or shake fruit from

BEN BERNARDS

the trees all around us, or grow food in the family garden. We lived in the traditional huts made from switchgrass and ironwood, with a handful of sheds and shacks serving as an open-air kitchen, dining room, gathering hall, and chapel.

It was another quiet evening in the jungle when Papa Aliki called out to us, an urgent edge in his voice. A young woman from our branch was with him, panting from fear and exhaustion. She'd come running through the jungle after hearing her father and the tribe's council of elders discussing a "problem" with the Mormons. As it turns out, they didn't care for strange, pudgy Americans like me coming into their tribe, with my horrible American accent, fancy clothes, and strange religious traditions, "stealing" away people from their faith. They felt like their traditions were being dishonored, and they decided it was time to "take care of the problem." At least, that's what the young girl had heard before she came running to warn us.

I didn't know for sure what "take care of us" really meant, but I sure could imagine all kinds of unpleasant ideas. *This can't be happening!* I thought to myself. *Weren't drunken mobs an old-fashioned thing that happened to "real" grown-ups? What had I done to them that would make them hate us? I've never been in a fight in my life!* (Well, unless you count my tackling my brother after a particularly vicious game of Mario Kart. But he totally deserved that.)

The girl warned us they'd be coming for us soon, possibly even that night. And if they decided to get drunk on their way over and arm themselves with torches and machetes, there would be no stopping their rampage.

So we circled up with the Alikis and planned our meager defenses. The boys sharpened their machetes and gave one each to my companion and me, telling us to keep the machetes close at all times. They sent the hunting dogs circling out around the huts in our clearing to scout out each of the trails leading to us. Then we gathered in a circle and offered a fervent prayer, pleading for protection. After feeling like we'd done all we could to prepare for that night, I retreated to my hut and sat in the dim light by the fire inside, trying to read

> *Weren't drunken mobs an old-fashioned thing that happened to "real" grown-ups?*

my scriptures, my journal, *anything* to keep my mind off the threats we were facing. My mind swirled with a mix of terror, panic, and resignation, realizing that there was a real possibility that I could die that night.

I have to admit that a part of me also felt angry at the world, like I'd somehow been cheated or tricked. I wanted to jump up and run out into the jungle, yelling to the sky *"I WASN'T READY FOR THIS! YOU NEVER TOLD ME THIS WAS GOING TO HAPPEN!"* When the anger cooled, it gave way to a fear of having been forsaken and forgotten. *Is this what a mission is really like?* I wondered. *Two whole years? Of this?* I had never considered the possibility of quitting my mission or asking to go home when life became difficult, but I'd be lying if I said that option didn't look really attractive right about then.

But deep in my heart, I knew that I couldn't give up. I had signed up for this—all of it—when I sent in my acceptance letter to President Gordon B. Hinckley and told him I would accept his call to serve. So I sat there in my hut that night, looking out into the darkness and trying not to imagine that I was seeing shadows of people moving through the trees.

And a wonderful thing happened.

A quiet sense of stillness and peace spread over my mind. It felt *solid*, like I could actually grab on and cling to it as a handhold in a blasting storm.

And I'll admit—that sense of stillness seemed so confusing and almost illogical. *How could I possibly be feeling calm right now?* I wondered. But the serenity was undeniable. There I was, tossed in the tempest of life-threatening persecution, bitterly calling out to my Master, wondering whether He even cared that I might perish. And I felt His answer: a simple, calm assurance that He not only cared, but He *knew* me, my companion, and the faithful family hosting us. He also knew what it was like to feel forsaken and threatened, for He had been there before. And it was that sense of divine empathy, of knowing that I wasn't alone in that moment of darkness, that somehow calmed my mind and assured me that everything would work out for the best. With that empathy came the understanding that His help would probably not come by stopping the murderous mob, but by giving me strength and resources to survive the[...]

I recalled the words of a country song that remind[...] though God can calm storms with a mere whisper, that[...] He always will do so whenever we ask Him to:[2]

> Sometimes He holds us close
> And lets the wind and waves go wild
> Sometimes He calms the storm
> And other times He calms His child

That night, two things became crystal clear: I was not abandoned by God in my darkest hour of despair, but neither was I immune from such darkness just because I was a missionary. Christ's peace would always be available to comfort me, but simply pleading for His help wouldn't "auto-magically" stop hard things from happening. Yes, His voice was powerful enough to cut through the storms of life and bring peace to my soul, but His love for me and desire for my progression meant He would let those storms continue to rage. Therefore I was left with a choice of where I would focus my faith: on my Master's voice, trusting that all would work out for my good, or on my fear of the pain I would experience along the way. Like Peter attempting to walk on stormy waters toward his Savior, I, too, could either keep my gaze fixed on God's light and promises or turn my eyes to the roiling waves and let the fear of failure overwhelm me.

I chose faith. And I felt something inside me change, as if my internal map was reoriented. I gained a new perspective on how God would help me overcome some troubles while others He would let me suffer from and grow from the experience. I realized that, yes, mortal dangers were going to be a common occurrence, just as they had been for countless missionaries around the world before me. Navigating my own stormy Galilee was the new normal. Hardships, even life-threatening, would be part of the deal. Because I'd offered to embark in the service of God, I would face obstacles to test my ability to serve with *all* my heart, might, mind, and strength. Those obstacles would be the heartbreaking but soul-building trials of missionary work. They would be monumentally difficult and intentionally stretch me past my perceived reaching point so that I might learn to rely on the outstretched hands of the Savior and His grace.

His heart aches with me as He allows me to suffer trials, and that same aching heart extends mercy that will help each of us to be strong enough to endure them, and to do so magnificently.

So trusting my all in His gentle care and knowing He loved me, I answered that night with heart sincere, *I'll be what you want me to be.* I grabbed my journal and started to write, thinking to myself, *This is not what they trained us for in Provo!*

Truth #1: It's going to be harder than you think.

THE OTHER SONS OF MOSIAH

The next few days were spent in restless anticipation, even after the calming peace we'd felt. For all we knew, the angry tribesmen were still out there, riled up and ready to attack. There was nothing I could do to stop them. We made sure to return to our huts early every night, which gave me lots of time to think and plan for the next day. I often wondered just what I had done to anger the natives. *Had we brought this on ourselves? Was this maybe a punishment due to lack of obedience, or did we just naively break some cultural taboo? Didn't our obedience and faith somehow qualify us for blessings that would have prevented all of this?* We were following the basic missionary formula of "follow the rules, open your mouth, work the vineyard, harvest the fruit, stay obedient, and return with honor," so why was this happening?

Truth #1: It's going to be harder than you think.

Years later, one of my students expressed the same frustration to me as we discussed his own mission experience. After a difficult battle with undiagnosed depression, he was honorably released and sent home to get the therapy he needed. Despite assurances that he'd done nothing wrong, he still felt that his mission had been a failure. He thought that if he had been obedient enough he could have somehow "faithed" his way out of depression. Or if God really loved him, He would have answered every prayer and fast and healed him. But of course it didn't turn out that way.

He later told me, "You know Bro. B, lots of people say their mission was the 'best two years of their lives,' but you don't often hear them say how *hard* it was, or that it was the *worst* two years or eighteen months of their lives.

"Nobody told me it was going to be this hard. Why not?!"

I wish I'd had a better answer for him at the time.

Later I was reading the story of Ammon among the Lamanites and a certain passage stuck out to me in a new way: "The Lord said unto them also: Go forth among the Lamanites, thy brethren, and establish my word; *yet ye shall be patient in long-suffering and afflictions*, that ye may show forth good examples unto them in me, and I will make an instrument of thee in my hands unto the salvation of many souls" (Alma 17:11; emphasis added).

God was telling them straight up that their afflictions (plural!) would require not just *some* suffering but *long*-suffering, and afflictions were incoming their direction. He was perfectly aware of how difficult their mission was going to be, and He was not about to smooth the road. He knew that "calm seas do not a sailor make."

I felt like I was on to something, so I dug further in to the scriptures to see if this pattern repeated, and sure enough I found story after story of honest, obedient, hardworking people who, despite all their faith and courage, still faced lives of trouble and misery: Nephi's murderous brothers (*and you thought* you *had family drama*), Abinadi's inflammatory speech against the king, Alma's disciples being burned in the martyrs' fire, all the way down to Moroni's decades-long solitary wanderings. Over and over again, the pattern of discipleship was made clear: men and women who enlist to serve their God will surely find success and triumph, but only at the cost of great struggle, transformational heartbreak, and enduring the dark nights of their own Gethsemanes.

In likening these stories to ourselves, it's natural to try to find an answer to the age-old question of "why do bad things happen to good people?" We were asked this question frequently as missionaries, especially when tragedy struck. We struggled to find satisfactory comfort for a grieving mother whose newborn had suddenly died from unexplained causes, or a father who was caught in a violent storm while fishing in the open sea, or the young woman whose family had disowned her for being baptized. Many times the only answer we could offer was that people had their agency or that the laws of nature couldn't be overruled. But sometimes we had no other response than a compassionate hug and an admittance that much of life is random and the dice don't always fall in our favor.

This appears to be the case with the *other* sons of Mosiah, Aaron and his brothers. You know the ones—while Ammon was winning the king's favor with his disarming personality and receiving offers of marriage, his brothers found a less-than-welcome reception in the next tribe over and were mocked, captured, tortured, imprisoned, and left to die. After their deliverance from prison, Mormon doesn't try to explain away their suffering or justify why it happened. He simply admits that "it was their lot to have fallen into the hands of a more hardened and a more stiffnecked people" (Alma 20:30)—it was an unlucky roll of the dice. We needn't suppose that Aaron and his brothers were any less valiant or faithful than Ammon, nor that their imprisonment was divine punishment or God's disapproval.

So yes, sometimes life is just hard, and sometimes it's just not fair.

CHALLENGED IN YOUR OWN WAY

But the good news is that whatever the cause of our troubles, every setback gives us the opportunity for refinement, a chance for meaningful growth, and invites us to drink deeper of spiritual waters. The peace of Christ is not always to be found in the *prevention* of difficulty but is frequently only obtained by gaining perspective while *enduring* such difficulties, and often more than once. The peace of perspective comes as we learn that the very roughness of the upward climb provides us the traction required to progress.

The trials that you will face as a missionary won't likely be from angry jungle mobs or any sort of significant physical danger. In fact, most missionaries report their biggest trial is the emotional and psychological shock of sudden, drastic, and relentless exposure to The New. New missionary routines, seemingly endless new rules, possibly even a new language, culture, and foods are all difficult challenges to face. Perhaps you'll be anxious about interacting with strangers face-to-face or leading groups of missionaries and members or speaking in public. You'll probably have to solve problems without receiving clear directions or face unprecedented challenges with very little assistance. Perhaps you'll be burdened by physical or mental health issues, financial difficulties, or family stresses from home. Chances are you'll have at least one companion with whom you just won't get along—someone who is different from you in personality, testimony, emotional maturity, life experience, degree of obedience, or desire to work. Perhaps your challenge will be that you won't "click" well with the members in your area or your mission president. You might feel lonely, forsaken, or homesick, and odds are at some point, you will question whether you really even want to be there. Or you may be one of the many who faithfully labor in all diligence while quietly questioning their faith and testimony in silence. (*I haven't scared you away yet, have I?*)

No matter what your trial, please hold to the knowledge that you are not alone in your agony nor will you fail in your attempts to endure. God knows you and loves you enough to allow you be stretched, even in uncomfortable ways. Let your faith be as Nephi, who knew that God only asks of us that which is possible, even though it is often difficult. Let your faith be like Paul and remember that God won't try us above what which we can bear. And let your

> **God knows you and loves you enough to allow you be stretched, even in uncomfortable ways.**

faith be like that of Alma's, who knew that while your faith may feel smaller than a grain of sand—just a particle—it can be carefully, patiently nourished and will eventually grow into a mighty, sturdy testimony.

To illustrate this point, consider a gem smith crafting a piece of fine jewelry. With an eye of faith, she patiently sifts through the roughest of raw materials, selecting stones that others may have overlooked as flawed, dull, or worthless. She cautiously cuts the rough rock down to a pre-form shape using high-powered diamond-tipped saw blades. Then she chooses progressively finer sanding tools to remove the lumpy outer layers and exposes the brilliant inner core. She carefully slices off unbalanced edges, cuts mathematically precise facets, and casts away everything that darkens and dulls the stone. After hours of intensive, delicate work, the final product is tested with bright white light. If the facet angles are properly aligned and the surfaces well polished, the shape of the newly crafted gem will not only accept the light but will reflect and amplify it, and it will gleam brilliantly.

Joseph Smith once said, "I am like a huge, rough stone rolling down from a high mountain; and the only polishing I get is when some corner gets rubbed off by coming in contact with something else, striking with accelerated force against religious bigotry, priest-craft, lawyer-craft, doctor-craft, lying editors, suborned judges and jurors, and the authority of perjured executives, backed by mobs, blasphemers, licentious and corrupt men and women—all hell knocking off a corner here and a corner there. Thus I will become a smooth and polished shaft in the quiver of the Almighty."[3]

My young friend, please remember that during hard times, when you may feel only pain, the Lord sees potential. Where you may suffer repeated trials, the Lord promises triumph. And whenever you endure the loneliness of tribulation, remember that God asks you to view it as the bitter sweetness of transformation. It is only by facing squarely the grinding surfaces of life that you may become the refined instrument that God needs. His power and patience can alchemize the darkest moments of your life into the most brilliant of blessings. As Thomas S. Monson said, "Our most significant opportunities will be found in times of greatest difficulty."[4]

WAITING IT OUT V. ENDURING IN FAITH

Gordon B. Hinckley had this to say about dealing with trials: "Get on your knees and ask for the blessings of the Lord; then stand on your feet and do what you are asked to do. Then leave the matter in the hands of the Lord."[5] It may sound like a paradox, but from my experience that quote truly captures the interdependence of a healthy relationship with God. So when trials come, and come they will, please hold on to all you've been taught and just keep going, knowing that each struggling step will lift you onward, upward, and forward. "Enduring in faith" means exercising all *your* power (or as the scriptures say, "heart, might, mind, and strength") to solve your own problems, move your own mountains, and walk yourself to Zion, while simultaneously embracing the belief that God will strengthen you along the way and consecrate your efforts.

Enduring to the end is not merely about "waiting it out" and counting down the days for your trials (or your mission) to be over. It's about *becoming*; it's about allowing God to shape you while you endure. It requires great humility to allow it to happen, and God won't override your agency in the process if you insist on resisting. Laman and Lemuel hiked the same boring desert as Nephi and Sam, but only the latter two were closer to God by the end of their journey. One pair of brothers complained about the difficulty of the task and whined that God should be delivering *them*, while the other pair dug in, carved their own way to the land Bountiful, and thanked God for the strength that made it possible.

There will likely be times when trials and discomforts are overwhelming and faith will falter—be it that of your companions, your members, your investigators, or even yourself. When the scaffolding of testimony wobbles or even falls to pieces under pressure, please have charity and patient kindness toward those who struggle—including yourself—for nobody is exempt such difficulties. To be a believer is to have your beliefs tested. So whether you are reaching out in empathy to someone who is struggling, or whether you yourself are desperately pleading to the heavens for an angel to come to strengthen you in *your* Gethsemane, know that you haven't been forsaken, that you will emerge triumphant from the testing and will have gained a deeper understanding, a loftier perspective, and broader empathy for those who struggle. You will develop great power to overcome challenges and courageous resolve to face whatever life may throw at you. You will be able to testify from personal experience that God was not only aware of you in the midst of *your* raging tempest, but that He *didn't* stop it on your behalf. Your voice will echo the confidence of Louisa May Alcott, who wrote, "I am not afraid of storms, for I am learning how to sail my ship."[6]

Finally, the simplest reminder of this principle may be found in the words spoken to Joseph Smith, huddled for months in the frigid dungeon of Liberty Jail. "O Lord, how long shall they suffer these wrongs?" he cried out in despair. After weeks of spiritual darkness finally came these calming words: "My son, peace be unto thy soul; thine adversity and thine afflictions shall be but a small moment; And then, *if thou endure it **well***, God shall exalt thee on high. . . .

Know thou, my son, that *all these things shall give thee experience, and shall be for thy good.* The Son of Man hath descended below them all. Art thou greater than he? Therefore, *hold on thy way*" (D&C 121:3, 7–8, 122:7–9; emphasis added).

Sometimes you'll find yourself in a dark place and feel like you've been buried—but perhaps you've only just been planted. When all of creation is crushing down on you, feel out to that inner, upward call to light and life and growth and know that as you keep pushing and sinking your roots into the soil of truth, you'll eventually break through above. And while most of your enduring growth may be unnoticeable and borne in loneliness, please remember that God's silence is not a sign of abandonment, for the Teacher is always quiet during the test.

Yes, no doubt about it—**a mission is going to be harder than you think, but it's possible with God's help**.

The scriptures tell us there must be opposition in all things, for without it we could not discern the sweet from the bitter. Would the marathon runner feel the triumph of finishing the race had she not felt the pain of the hours of pushing against her limits? Would the pianist feel the joy of mastering an intricate sonata without the painstaking hours of practice?

In stories, as in life, adversity teaches us things we cannot learn otherwise. Adversity helps to develop a depth of character that comes in no other way. Our loving Heavenly Father has set us in a world filled with challenges and trials so that we, through opposition, can learn wisdom, become stronger, and experience joy.

–President Dieter F. Uchtdorf[7]

TRUTH #2

Evil Is Real, but God Is More Powerful

"The world will war against you; the devil will,
earth will, and hell will.
But you must bear testimony of me.
You must preach the Gospel, do your duty,
and the Lord will stand by you.
Earth and hell shall not prevail against you."

—Joseph Smith[8]

CHASED FROM MU

Life in the jungle was sweet in its simplicity. We followed the schedule of nature: rising with the dawn and retiring at sunset, cooking over open fires whatever we could fish from the sea, shake out of a tree, pull from the ground, or catch in a snare. We became part of our tribe by working with them in their fields, tending their animals, and helping build their huts. We were able to expand our influence with other tribes by performing *la coutume*[9] whenever we visited new tribes or influential families.

And we learned that all these efforts to build up goodwill and trust could be dashed to pieces in a moment.

One day a young man from the neighboring tribe of Mu was visiting some friends in our tribe. He'd heard of us Mormon missionaries and approached us with a question: "Do you guys believe in visions?"

I thought he was joking. *That's not the kind of question you get every day!* I thought to myself, looking at my companion for direction. He kindly smiled and nodded at the man and answered, "We sure do."

"Good!" said the man. "My brother Christopher had a vision of God, but nobody in our tribe believes him, not even our pastor. Could you come talk to him?"

We agreed to visit him and set an appointment. But something about the whole episode troubled me.

"Elder," I asked my companion, "you don't *really* believe that God would just appear to some random guy out on this island, do you?"

He smiled at me patiently. "Come on, Elder Bernards," he said. "If God could appear to a 1800s teenage farm boy, couldn't he appear to a 1900s teenage island boy?"

Fair enough, I thought, chagrined.

The day of our appointment came, and we brought along one of our members named Gaspard as a tribal escort. We hoped he would help us gain favor with the family and the Mu tribespeople. We'd never taught there before, and even though we had permission from the chief, we were still considered outsiders.

We arrived at the family's home and I noticed immediately that something felt *off*. I couldn't tell if I was just imagining it or feeling nervous, so I checked with my companion and he shared my concern. His face was calm and collected, but as his eyes met mine I could see the worry. *He's feeling it too*, I realized. *Something's not right here.*

"This may be a bit of a challenge," my companion muttered under his breath in quiet English. "Gaspard just told me that their father is the tribe's pastor, and they are *very* defensive about their faith. Stay on your toes and follow the Spirit."

I said a silent prayer in my heart that we'd be able to do just that: that we'd be safe, and that their hearts would be softened. Just then, a young man with kind eyes and a gentle smile appeared from the home and greeted us warmly, shaking our hands. This was Christopher, the boy who'd seen the vision. He seemed friendly and curious about us Americans, and I instantly felt safe with him.

Whatever was bothering us about this visit, it wasn't stemming from him. He sat with me at one end of the table, while his older brother and mother sat by my companion and Gaspard at the other end.

We exchanged pleasantries and asked Christopher to share his story. He said that he was sitting on the beach recently, thinking about life, when a Being of light appeared in the sky and spoke to him. He felt filled with light and love and finally knew for himself that God existed, but there was still so much more he wanted to learn. When he shared the experience with other people at his church, however, he was ridiculed and told "visions didn't happen anymore." (*Sound familiar?*)

He looked at me earnestly and asked "What do *you* guys think? Is it real?"

My companion nodded to me, so I took a deep breath and replied. "God certainly could appear to anyone today, just as He has done many times in the past. We may not be able to explain everything about that vision, but there are some other things about God and His plan for us that we *can* teach. Could we share a story similar to yours, about another boy with a vision?"

They nodded and we felt a moment of relief. *Perhaps my uneasy foreboding was a false alarm after all*, I thought.

So I started the story of Joseph Smith's First Vision.

And that's when things started to get *weird*.

The mother and brother started muttering and making comments to Gaspard in their native tongue, and he replied to them politely, translating for my companion along the way. Something was upsetting them, and they weren't really even listening to my conversation with Christopher. Gaspard was trying to keep them calm and the situation under control, but their anger continued to escalate. I paused my discussion with Christopher and looked at my companion. He motioned for me to continue while he addressed their concerns at the other end of the table.

So Christopher and I locked eyes with each other and I worked my way through the discussion, nervously glancing at the brother and mother as we heard their voices raise in anger. And that's when we felt it: the strange sense of *wrong* we'd first felt upon arrival seemed to concentrate in an invisible cloud of darkness above the mother and son at the other end of the table. We could feel it growing stronger around them, amplifying their agitation while I testified of truth. Christopher and I seemed caught in our own little bubble of calm as I unfolded the story of the Restoration and Joseph's First Vision while the cloud of darkness swelled out around my companion and Gaspard and the rest of the family. We could feel the two sides pressing against each other in a sort of spiritual tug-of-war. The darkness seemed to prevail as their anger grew and voices escalated.

I stumbled over my final words to Christopher, my tongue thick with anxiety as I struggled with the language and tried to speak calmly and bear a final testimony. The family was now shouting at my companion, who still calmly rebuffed their arguments, but I could tell from his urgent glances at me that our time was up and we needed to leave.

"Christopher!" I half-yelled, smiling at him as I snapped him back to attention. He startled, realizing he'd been watching the arguing at the other end, feeling the energy of both sides swelling to a bursting point. He looked back at me as I asked my final question: "Christopher, do you believe it?"

"Do you believe it?"

The words seemed to hang in the air and his eyes grew distant, as if something inside him was resonating to a long-forgotten tune. The other end of the table hadn't heard what I'd said, but they'd suddenly grown quiet. For a split second, everything paused and the world fell still.

Then Christopher broke into a smile. "*YES!*" he exclaimed. "Yes! It's true. I feel it in my heart."

He threw his head back in childish innocence and laughed. I didn't realize I'd been holding my breath all this time until I let it all out in a sigh of relief, laughing with him. *Oh merci Dieu!* I thought, thanking God that we had made it to the end and accomplished what we'd been sent to do.

And then all hell broke loose.

The cloud of darkness finally burst over the table in a fit of yelling and rage as the brother finally let loose and yelled for us to leave, slamming the table with his fists and knocking a book to the floor. He snapped at his mother, who disappeared inside with the other children, fearful of his anger. The protective bubble of calm around Christopher and me disappeared with a pop and we knew that was our cue to get out *now*. So we gathered our scattered materials, thanked them for their hospitality, and hustled to our car.

"Elder Bernards, as soon as we're clear of the house, *floor* it back to our tribe and don't stop for anything!" my companion whispered to me as we piled in and started the engine. "We need to get out of here *now*."

And that's when we felt it—the darkness that had surrounded the brother now seemed to detach from him and was bubbling out toward us. We couldn't *see* anything exactly, but an unmistakable sensation of fear and evil was emanating out from their house and chasing us as we sped away into the jungle toward our tribe and safety. I sped off through the dark misty jungle, my companion urging me to go faster while Gaspard mumbled prayers in his native tongue. We could feel the surging cloud chasing us along the road and I probably ran over a chicken or two on the way out the tribe, but I didn't care—I just wanted to get away.

Back in our tribe, we finally skidded to a stop in front of our hut, leapt from the car, and ran inside, tripping over each other as we collapsed on the woven floor mats. Whatever had been chasing us finally dissipated once we crossed into the Aliki family grounds, leaving us in our quiet corner of the jungle alone.

We lay on the floor catching our breath, goose-bumped and scared out of our skins but alive. A small fire was crackling low and inviting, and steam curled gently off the grass walls. "What was *that*?" I finally asked no one in particular, still stunned from the harrowing chase we'd just endured. My companion murmured a prayer of thanksgiving, opened his eyes and stared upward at the ceiling. He waited a long time before answering me.

"That, Elder, was the adversary. Now you know."

Truth #2: Evil is real.

WHAT JOSEPH LEARNED THAT DAY

Spoiler alert: we were never able to go back to Mu, nor able teach

Christopher again. News travels fast through the tribes, especially when it's the angry brother's version of what he claimed happened during our visit. Word spread that we had supposedly offended the family and insulted their traditions. The Alikis counseled us to never cross into that tribe again, for if we did and we were caught, we probably wouldn't leave alive.

Truth #2: Evil is real.

As frightening as that experience was, I couldn't help but see the parallels between our experience and the story recounted by young Joseph Smith. You remember how the story goes, right? When he went off into the woods to try to figure out just what he believed? He learned a hard lesson about threats unseen too.

In his own words,

> After I had retired to the place where I had previously designed to go, having looked around me, and finding myself alone, I kneeled down and began to offer up the desires of my heart to God. I had scarcely done so, when immediately I was seized upon by some power which entirely overcame me, and had such an astonishing influence over me as to bind my tongue so that I could not speak. Thick darkness gathered around me, and it seemed to me for a time as if I were doomed to sudden destruction. (Joseph Smith—History 1:15)

His experience illustrates a simple fact: evil truly exists and will frequently attempt to stop us from getting closer to God. This may be a weird concept for me to have a testimony of, but I can say that I know for myself that the enemy of our souls is real, that he has spokespeople in every corner of the world, and that they are actively engaged in a campaign of spiritual warfare against those who choose to follow God and His Christ. Some of us may go our entire lives without feeling a direct and open assault like I experienced, while others may feel buffeted on a regular basis. Either way, there is truth in Joseph Smith's comment that "the nearer a person approaches the Lord, a greater power will be manifested by the Adversary to prevent the accomplishment of His purposes."[10]

Sometimes the adversary will have great success in disguising his very existence, flattering people away, . . . telling them there is no hell nor devil (see 2 Nephi 28:22). While other times he'll reverse his tactics, throw off all concealment, and openly manifest himself for the world to see. But no matter how he strives against us, the Light of Christ is powerful enough to shine through the darkness of Satan's lies and illusions and reveal them for the deceptions they are. Hence the need for members and missionaries alike to strive to keep the Spirit in their lives, so they may "search diligently in the light of Christ" and be able to "know good from evil" (Moroni 7:19).

Among the many things Joseph learned that day in the grove, he became painfully aware that the battle for our souls, begun in the premortal life, continues to rage now—if only on a different battle-field. Yes, there is a God in heaven who hears and answers prayers. And so too is there an adversary who often times will do everything possible to prevent us from communicating with that loving Father. Satan knew that if Joseph were able to talk with God that day, the world would never be the same. It's no surprise then that he unleashed the full might of his power to try to stop such a glorious event from happening.

YOU'RE GETTING WARMER

I noticed a similar pattern in the lives of friends who were waiting to report to the MTC. A surprising number of them kept experiencing regular episodes of increased struggle and temptations in the weeks preceding their departure for duty. Sure, some of these new problems could have been explained away as random coincidence or stress, but quite a few of them were clearly moments of unusual darkness, contention, and strife. Some greater, unseen power seemed to be determined to hinder their spiritual growth.

One moment was particularly somber for me as I saw one of my brothers fight this same sort of battle. A few weeks before he left for the Provo MTC, he got into what should have been a minor disagreement with my mother, only to flip into an uncharacteristic rage and storm out of the house. I approached my mom in confusion. "What the heck is his problem?" I asked. "Why has he been getting angry so much lately?"

She smiled sadly and patiently replied, "The Lord is about to get a new missionary soon. You don't think Satan is just going to sit back and let that happen, now do you?"

Well, that would explain it, I thought, feeling a bit more empathy for him. Surely he was already under enough stress and anxiety at the prospect of leaving his family and friends for two years, and he seemed to only get worse as the great deceiver kept up his campaign to "rage in the hearts of men" (2 Nephi 28:20).

This pattern became recognizable in too many of my friends. It was as if the greatest tempting pressure barreled down on them like an avalanche during those few weeks or months between receiving their mission call and actually reporting to the MTC. It felt like the closer they got to their day of departure, the enemy turned up the heat and tried to trip them up, give it up, knock them down, or push them aside. He actually succeeded with a few of them, sadly.

James E. Faust said, "You must know that Lucifer will oppose you, and be prepared for his opposition. Do not be surprised. He wants you to fail. Discouragement is one of the devil's tools. Have courage and go forward. Recognize that the gospel has been preached with some pain and sorrow from the very beginning of time. Do not expect that your experience will be otherwise."[11]

As missionaries we learned how to recognize this pattern and anticipate the challenges that came with increased spiritual light. Any time we seemed to make a little progress with investigators we would inevitably experience an increase in stormy spiritual weather. In anticipation of such opposition, we decided to counsel with our branch members and fellow missionaries and preemptively devise strategies to reinforce the faith of our investigators and help them weather the storms that were sure to come. We knew that because they were striving to come unto Christ and build their spiritual foundation upon the rock of His gospel, we could anticipate the devil to send forth mighty winds, whirlwind-driven shafts, blinding hail and mighty storms to stop them up in their journey (see Helaman 5:12). But we also knew if we did everything in our power to endure in faith, to hold onto the covenants we had made (or were *going* to make), that storm would have no power over us or our investigators. So we made sure we checked in daily with our investigators, we enlisted the help of as many Church auxiliaries as we could to extend the circle of friendship to these new strangers, and we regularly taught them simple, actionable Church doctrines and invited them to act on those truths and learn for themselves that they were true. We prayed with them, we fasted with them, and we feasted together on the words of Christ, linked arm in arm as we bravely faced down the storms of life that raged around them.

Yes, a disciple's journey to Christ will always be an uphill climb. But that struggle itself is a sign that we are heading in the right direction.

WHAT MOSES LEARNED THAT DAY

Elsewhere in the scriptures we see another tactic Satan uses that is quite the opposite of what he tried to do to young Joseph. If the adversary fails to *prevent* us from coming closer to God, he'll frequently resort to his next-best tactic: cheapen the spiritual experience, weaken its impression on our minds, and deaden our sensitivity to its importance.

Consider the story of Moses as found in the Pearl of Great Price. There we read of the former prince of Egypt, now exiled and shepherding in a faraway desert with a new adopted family. Traumatized by the loss of his royal identity and heritage, he now struggles to find purpose, family, and a direction for his new life. After an initial miraculous encounter with Jehovah calling to him from the midst of a burning bush, he is once again caught up into the top of a mountain and there sees God face-to-face and hears His voice. There he is shown the full panorama of God's creation, divinely commissioned with a prophetic purpose, and is ultimately left to himself greatly marveling and wondering at it all (see Moses 1:8). But perhaps the most stunning thing he learns is that he is a literal descendent of that self-same Creator, endowed with all the rights, privileges, and possibilities that come with such a divine heritage. His lineage needn't be traced to his adopted bedouin family where he now lived, to the royal house of Pharaoh wherein he was raised, nor to the poor, courageous Hebrew slave mother who hid him in a basket as a baby. No, he learns that he is a direct offspring of the Creator of the universe, God, and is reminded of that boggling fact over and over again as God repeatedly calls him "my son." (*Wouldn't you find it hard to believe too?*) Where all the other gods of Egypt existed as shapeless pagan explanations of the natural world around them (floods, earthquakes, sunrise, life, and death, and so on), here Moses now had first-hand experience with the reality of the existence of a true Divine Being from a different realm. And what's more, that Being *knew Moses by name and identified him as His own kin.* No wonder that this new knowledge and perspective left him, just like young Joseph back in the grove, stunned and unmoving for hours, his mind reeling with new perspective and understanding. He finally comes to his senses and utters perhaps the greatest understatement in the scriptures: "Now, for this cause I know that man is nothing, which thing I never had supposed" (Moses 1:10). Moses isn't denigrating himself or criticizing his species, but rather he realizes that mortal man, on his own, is nothing compared to the exalted majesty that awaits the faithful who live up to their birthright. The glorious monuments of Egyptian royal dynasties pale in comparison to the endless creations of our Celestial King, and such creations would be our own if we continue in the paths of righteousness. That is our inheritance, our legacy, and our destiny.

No surprise, then, to see who would appear immediately after this glorious revelation. "When Moses had said these words, behold, Satan came tempting him, saying: Moses, *son of man*, worship me" (Moses 1:12; emphasis added).

Can you believe the sheer *nerve* of that guy? Showing up once the celestial light started to fade, and not even bothering to tempt Moses with such typical empty promises of riches, power, or prestige. No, Satan directly attacks that which was most precious to Moses: his new knowledge of his relationship with God and his freshly revealed divine heritage. Can't you almost hear the derision dripping from Satan's voice, referring to him as nothing more than a "son of man" while insisting that *he* was the Only Begotten and fit for Moses's worship? But Moses knows better. He sees through the deception, and (after Satan throws a tantrum worthy of an over-sugared Sunbeam class) dismisses him without a moment's consideration of Satan's counterfeit offerings.

The adversary uses this technique—showing up right after we experience "spiritual highs" in an attempt to dissolve and dilute them—quite frequently and to good effect. (He has had millennia to practice, after all.) He'll often try to slide into our thoughts at an opportune time, scattering seeds of doubt in the freshly furrowed soil of the heart alongside the newly sown seeds of testimony. He will nourish those doubts with fear, lies, and half-truths, hoping to quickly choke out the budding testimony before it grows.

This tactic is also illustrated elsewhere in the scriptures, in Lehi's vision of the tree of life. There he "beheld others pressing forward, and they came forth and caught hold of the end of the rod of iron; and they did press forward through the mist of darkness, clinging to the rod of iron, even until they did come forth and partake of the fruit of the tree. *And after they had partaken of the fruit of the tree they did cast their eyes about as if they were ashamed*" (1 Nephi 8:24–25; emphasis added). It wasn't the fruit that brought the shame, but the voices of sin, doubt, and mockery, shouting from the great and spacious building that came after they had a chance to taste of that fruit, sweeter than all else. The volume of the mockery was just loud enough, the message just strong enough to overpower the joy of those who, not seconds before, had tasted of the love of God.

If Satan can't stop you from getting close to God, sometimes he'll try to convince you that it wasn't worth it, that it wasn't real, or that it won't last. If he can't prevent you from hearing God's message of complete truth, he'll patiently wait his turn to overwhelm you with counterfeit half-truths, cleverly packaged and enticingly presented and designed to flood you with so many questions and doubts that you'll feel powerless to address every one of them. *"And even if you were to do so, what use is there of building up such faith when it may ultimately be torn down again?"* he asks. He may not always be able to prevent you from feeling the Spirit, but he certainly will not cease attacking you after you do. With so much potential good that you can do as a disciple of Christ and faithful missionary, with so much on the line in the lives of your investigators as they are about to change their eternal direction and finally adjust to a heading pointing to God, it's no wonder that the adversary would seek out every opportunity to cheapen, poison, demean, or belittle your righteous experiences. He believes that if he can convince even one of us that we are no longer the glorious sons

[Satan will] try to convince you that it wasn't worth it, that it wasn't real, or that it won't last.

and daughters of God as Moses saw, but are mere children of men with no potential or power, then he wins.

EVIL IS REAL, BUT GOD IS MORE POWERFUL

These two tactics—either trying to stop us from coming closer to God or trying to spoil the experience afterward—are instructive bookends about Satan's strategies. Within them we find the entire breadth of his overall plan: to ultimately separate us from God and from each other. Where God's work and glory is our eternal life and exalted union, the enemy's undertaking is our eternal spiritual death and ultimate solitude. That is his goal for us, for that is also his own doom. Knowing full well what awaits him, his endeavor is to drag down with him all the souls he can, "for he seeketh that all men might be miserable like unto himself" (2 Nephi 2:27). But regardless of which tactic he employs, he can be thwarted at every step by the same counter-response: by calling upon the powers of heaven to rebuff, rebuke, and dismiss the enemy. Notice the similarities in Joseph's and Moses's responses:

> But, *exerting all my powers to call upon God* to deliver me out of the power of this enemy which had seized upon me, and at the very moment when I was ready to sink into despair and abandon myself to destruction—not to an imaginary ruin, but to the power of some actual being from the unseen world, who had such marvelous power as I had never before felt in any being—just at this moment of great alarm, I saw a pillar of light exactly over my head, above the brightness of the sun, which descended gradually until it fell upon me.
>
> It no sooner appeared than *I found myself delivered from the enemy* which held me bound. (Joseph Smith—History 1:16–17; emphasis added)

> Moses began to fear exceedingly; and as he began to fear, he saw the bitterness of hell. Nevertheless, *calling upon God*, he received strength, and he commanded, saying: Depart from me, Satan, for this one God only will I worship, which is the God of glory.
>
> And now Satan began to tremble, and the earth shook; and Moses received strength, and called upon God, saying: In the name of the Only Begotten, depart hence, Satan.
>
> And it came to pass that Satan cried with a loud voice, with

weeping, and wailing, and gnashing of teeth; and *he departed hence*, even from the presence of Moses, that he beheld him not. (Moses 1:20–22; emphasis added)

No matter how he rants and raves, Satan simply cannot withstand the commanding power of Jesus Christ, nor any faithful man or woman, boy or girl, speaking in His name. The adversary may unleash every attack conceivable to hinder our journey back to God. He may craft the most cunning deceit to cheapen, counterfeit, and diminish one's newly granted celestial light. But all his machinations will ultimately fall to pieces under the authority of the God of heaven. Those who hold on and hope on, even at faith's uttermost edge, will be able to proclaim like Nephi of old that "God hath been [their] support; he hath led [them] through [their] afflictions in the wilderness; and he hath preserved [them] upon the waters of the great deep" (2 Nephi 4:20).

There are a handful of effective ways to regain control over him and nullify his temptations, many of which you've probably heard from your youth. Hymns and songs sung both vocally and in the heart, recited quotes or scriptures (now you know one reason for all those scripture masteries in seminary!), and inspirational stories are all useful for resetting your internal spiritual light. You can use them anywhere, anytime, and you are only limited by how much you are willing to memorize. The greater your mental arsenal, the more prepared you'll be when the enemy's power assails you.

Here are some additional ideas on how to keep the Spirit of the gospel burning strong in your heart and mind:

- Print out copies of your mission's favorite "theme" scripture and tack them on the walls, reciting it out loud on a regular basis. Write up the scripture from your missionary plaque or other favorite scripture masteries and post them around your flat (apartment).
- Carry small flashcards with the text of verses you'd like to memorize and spend downtime committing them to memory. You'd be amazed at how many chances you have to do this while riding in a car, waiting for meetings to start, or in between appointments.

- Select a scripture to memorize and ponder during your companionship study, and make it a point of focus for a whole week.
- Fill your flat with inspirational art. Church magazines are excellent sources of visual content. Share the images freely with your members and investigators too. We made it a tradition to gift new members images of the Savior or temples to hang in their homes as a way of helping them be reminded of the covenants they made.
- Carry with you external mementos of spiritual significance. These could be the traditional CTR rings, Young Women medallions, or other tokens of remembrance. For some it may be a particular souvenir of a girls' camp or Young Men trek, or other artifact that is tied to a spiritual highlight of your life. (My personal favorites are a handkerchief from my local temple dedication and a smooth stone from a monumental seminary lesson on my last day of high school. Every time I physically reconnected with them, I likewise spiritually reconnected with how I felt on those occasions.)

So remember that story from chapter 1, about the neighboring tribesmen who were going to come attack us? Or the story of getting chased out of Mu by some unseen force of evil? They both have something incredible in common: in each instance, we cried out in fearful desperation for help, and help was given in miraculous ways.

Even though we were chased by a being of evil from the tribe of Mu, it was stopped that night from entering into our home. I personally believe it could not come onto the holy ground that the Aliki family had established in their home. (Seriously, it was like a force-field around our hut that night!) As for the angry tribesmen—well, let's just say that deliverance came from a very surprising source (stay tuned for chapter 3—it was pretty amazing).

No matter what form your trials may take, rest assured that God is aware of you, for you are on His errand and He will not leave you unwatched. He has given you ways to thwart the power of the enemy, and we've listed a few of them here. Be mindful of His promise that He will be on your right hand, and on your left, and His angels will be round about you to bear you up, and you will find additional ways to dispel the darkness from your life, and the lives of those you teach (see D&C 84:88).

Yes, **evil is real, but God is more powerful**.

In 1980, a young man from Rwanda was forced by his tribe to either renounce Christ or face certain death. He refused to renounce Christ, and he was killed on the spot. The night before he had written the following commitment that was found in his room:

> I am a part of the fellowship of the Unashamed. I have the Holy Spirit of Power. The die has been cast. I have stepped over the line. The decision has been made. I am a disciple of Jesus Christ. I won't look back, let up, slow down, back away, or be still. My past is redeemed, my present makes sense, and my future is secure. I am finished and done with low living, sight walking, small planning, smooth knees, colorless dreams, tame visions, mundane talking, chintzy giving, and dwarfed goals.
>
> I no longer need preeminence, prosperity, position, promotions, plaudits, or popularity. I don't have to be right, first, tops, recognized, praised, regarded, or rewarded. I now live by presence, learn by faith, love by patience, lift by prayer, and labor by power.
>
> My pace is set, my gait is fast, my goal is Heaven, my road is narrow, my way is rough, my companions few, my Guide is reliable, my mission is clear. I cannot be bought, compromised, deterred, lured away, turned back, diluted, or delayed. I will not flinch in the face of sacrifice, hesitate in the presence of adversity, negotiate at the table of the enemy, ponder at the pool of popularity, or meander in the maze of mediocrity.
>
> I won't give up, back up, let up, or shut up until I've preached up, prayed up, paid up, stored up, and stayed up for the cause of Christ. I am a disciple of Jesus Christ. I must go until He returns, give until I drop, preach until all know, and work until He comes.
>
> And when He comes to get His own, He will have no problem recognizing me. My colors will be clear for "I am not ashamed of the Gospel, because it is the power of God for the salvation of everyone who believes (Romans 1:16).

–Dr. Bob Moorehead[12]

TRUTH #3

Miracles Happen, and They're Unlocked by Patient Obedience

"He manifesteth himself unto all those who believe in him, by the power of the Holy Ghost; yea, unto every nation, kindred, tongue, and people, working mighty miracles, signs, and wonders, among the children of men according to their faith."

–2 Nephi 26:13

GOD'S HIDDEN HAND

Several peaceful weeks passed in the Lifou jungle with no news or threats from the tribesmen, and we finally began to feel safe again. We had resumed our visits within the tribe and were even able to perform a welcoming *coutume* ceremony with a neighboring tribe's chief. He would now grant us permission to move freely within their boundaries and share our message with anyone who was interested. But even though the surface storms appeared to have calmed, tension and mistrust was still boiling within the hearts of many of the natives.

When the time came for our next missionary zone conference, we boarded a small plane and flew back to the mainland to join the other missionaries. While we were there we called up the Aliki family in Lifou to check on them and the branch members—and they had some very surprising news.

"Oh Elders, this is scary," Mama Aliki told my companion over the phone. "Yesterday, our tribe's pastor and his friends finally decided to come get you. We got a secret warning just in time and were able to gather up the branch members, hunker down in our huts, and pray to God for protection. That night the mob came, angry and ready to fight, looking for you Americans. We told them you had left and we didn't know when you would be back. They argued with Papa for a little bit but finally left us alone. It's a good thing you were gone!" What an amazing coincidence that we had meetings scheduled just then!

But just a month later, another similar "coincidence" occurred. By then I had a new companion and it was the season for tribal weddings, which usually meant weeks of partying, ceremonies, and very little successful missionary work. Once again someone in the tribes decided to stir up some trouble and rough up the Mormons a bit, and again the network of tribal contacts brought advance warning. (Pro tip: befriend the children in your area!) So again we bunkered down and laid low, hoping the threat would fizzle out unproductively. But one day my companion suddenly became violently ill and was diagnosed as having contracted an acute jungle infection. Within forty-eight hours he became so sick that we had to emergency evacuate him for treatment on the next plane back to the mainland.

And guess who happened to come looking for us while we were gone? Sure enough, the same angry natives once again tried storming the family compound, but the Americans were nowhere to be found.

Three times they came to attack, and three times we happened to be somewhere else. The first time we missed them, I could chalk up to random luck. But the second or third times . . . either the angry natives had *horrible* timing or perhaps there was some sort of divine intervention taking place behind the scenes. I'll probably never know for sure either way, but I like to believe that God's hidden help was there all along, quietly nudging the universe in our favor—yes, even through jungle infections.

I read somewhere that coincidence is just God's way of remaining anonymous. Your mission is probably going to be full of a multitude of similar occurrences, many of which could be given a logical explanation. Sometimes we'll never be sure of just how or when God influences our lives—maybe that's our

Truth #3: Miracles happen.

chance to grow a bit of humble faith as we live with that uncertainty. On rare occasions His handiwork is revealed in bold vibrant colors, with broad brushstrokes and sharp, heavy lines, clearly bearing His divine signature. Other times, perhaps most frequently, His tender mercies will be sketched in our lifebooks with only the faintest of outlines, nearly invisible watermarks, and the gentlest of embossings that can be felt by only the most sensitive of fingers. Perhaps He does so to allow us to *choose* to see it, or perhaps He stays mostly hidden as a way of allowing us to grow our faith in that which we don't fully see. Whatever the reasons, learning to recognize His touch in our lives and acknowledge His influence is a spiritual skill that is not developed overnight but requires a lifetime of study and practice. When a humble heart is paired with eyes to see and ears to hear, they will slowly begin to recognize the handiwork of He who has been carefully crafting behind our life-scenes all along. Where one may see ordinary coincidence, others can learn to see the miraculous fingerprints of God.

Truth #3: Miracles happen.

THE EFFECTUAL DOOR

"Elders and sisters, we have a problem," our mission president said as he looked over our small group of missionaries. We were clustered around rows of tables in a chapel's cultural hall, gathered for another zone conference. We'd gathered from all across the island, as we did every month when he flew in from Fiji to visit us.

Uh oh, I thought. *What did we do this time? Was it the office elders? I bet they finally got caught pranking his wife. Those guys think they can get away with anything!*

"Elders, there are no musicians in Fiji," he continued. "Or Vanuatu, or Wallis and Futuna, or any of the other islands in this mission. In fact, of the 160 plus missionaries assigned to the Fiji Islands mission, the *only* ones with any musical experience are right here, in New Caledonia. I can't even find people back on our island to play the piano for sacrament meeting. Do you know how *rare* it is for a Mormon congregation to have no piano players? It's unheard of!"

Everyone chuckled and looked at Elder St. Clair, our resident *maestro*. He was our go-to piano man. He could sight-read anything you put in front of him, improvise creative arrangements of well-known hymns, and had even started composing short songs as special musical numbers for baptisms.

"So I think the time has come to put this talent to use," the president continued. "If God put all the musical talent on this one island, maybe we need to start using it. Grab your scriptures and turn to Doctrine and Covenants 100:3."

I followed along as the president read out loud, "Behold, and lo, I have much people in this place, in the regions round about; and an effectual door shall be opened in the regions round about in this eastern land."

"Elders, I think it's time we open the 'effectual door' and your musical talents are going to be the key." He closed his scriptures and watched our expressions, which surely must have been pure bewilderment. "You know that the people here love their *kaneka*.[13] I want you to start talking to them in a 'language' they will understand. You need to start speaking to them more through music. Yes, I know you've already done a handful of missionary musical numbers and small choruses for firesides and such, but I think it's time for you to stretch yourselves in a new direction. I'd like you to start asking members and their friends if anyone has instruments you can borrow. I'd like you to start using some proselyting time to write new songs and practice as a group—any missionary with musical talent can help out. And if you can't sing or play anything, you can help out in supporting roles, like organizing performances and helping with productions. Everyone can put their shoulder to the wheel in their own way."

We shifted in our seats and chuckled uncomfortably, unsure of what he was suggesting.

"Uh, President?" One of the zone leaders raised his hand. "What are we supposed to do exactly? Do you want us to, like, start a band?"

The mission president smiled warmly.

"That's exactly right, Elder. I want you to start a band."

DRESSED IN WHITE

The next few weeks were a frantic flurry of creative excitement as we were turned loose in this new venture. Christmas was only a few weeks away, so we decided that that would be our chance to debut a traveling missionary choir. Elder St. Clair of course would be our chief pianist. Elder Smatti was on a borrowed guitar. Elder Mongas happened to play jazz saxophone, so he emailed his parents and they shipped him his horn all the way from France. I joined a few elders and the sisters in the chorus and we started creating our own arrangements of holiday songs, since there wasn't much sheet music to be found on the island.

> "That's exactly right, Elder. I want you to start a band."

One song in particular had a cool backstory: I had been in the MTC during the Christmas season and we naturally had spent a lot of time singing every holiday song known to man and Mormon. One day a teacher of mine approached me out of the blue with sheet music in her hand—a special arrangement of the beloved French hymn "O Holy Night." She handed it to me and said, "I don't really know why, but I feel that you could use this or that it might come in handy on your mission." Little did she know what a blessing it would be for us to have that song. A whole year later, when we were faced with a daunting task and had no money to buy sheet music and the island had no internet access, I dug through my suitcases, found that one arrangement, and it became one of our signature performance pieces.

Other missionaries started finding creative ways to contribute as well, using talents and skills from their pre-mission life that they had no idea would come in handy in the field. Elder DeOliveira, who was a music producer and sound engineer before coming to the islands, had naturally befriended an inactive member that was part of a rock band with their own recording studio. Not only did the band offer to let us use their studio for rehearsals, but they loaned us mixing boards, amps, speakers, cables, microphones, and any other sound gear we needed. A few guys from the elders quorum became our "roadies" and volunteered to lug around all the sound equipment needed for each performance. Our jolly Elder Hatch was a natural fit to be Santa Claus, so one of the Relief Societies sewed a full Santa suit for him and he became our Christmas choir mascot. The rest of the elders started contacting each branch and district presidency, asking for opportunities to bring our Christmas musical message to their people. We were not yet the full band that the mission president had envisioned, but we were on our way.

And the doors started opening.

Members started donating even more sheet music, office supplies, decorations, and inviting us to their branches to sing in sacrament meetings. We were able to perform at shopping centers, malls, and even the town's main square. A sister from one of our branches worked in a retirement home and was able to get permission for us to visit and perform for the widows there. Another brother had contacts at a remote orphanage and invited us to visit the children as a special holiday surprise. We came bearing simple gifts and treats, but more importantly we brought love, kindness, and one-on-one attention to the young children there who rarely had loving, personal contact.

And then one day we got a drummer, and everything changed.

His name was Elder Roberts, and as soon as he arrived at the mission office, we asked if he had any musical talent he'd like to share. We told him that we'd been traveling around and performing Christmas songs but were looking to expand our reach in new ways. "Well, yeah, I was in a ska band before my mission, played the drums," he replied, somewhat puzzled. "But why? It's not like you're going to start a rock band or anything like that, are you?"

My companion grinned at me as the wheels in our heads started spinning with new ideas. "Actually, Elder, we just may do that," I replied, wrapping an arm around his shoulders. "Let's introduce you to the rest of our group."

The other missionaries warmly accepted our new band member and we changed gears from holiday/spiritual tunes to contemporary Christian rock. A member family donated a bass guitar and amp and taught Elder Groberg how to play. Elder St. Clair started writing new songs, and soon we had a dozen pop anthems about life as a missionary and disciple of Christ. Our friend with the studio volunteered his recording time and helped us produce and cut our one and only LP under the band name "Dressed In White." Our signature white shirts, ties, and missionary name tags graced the album cover art with a sketch of an electric guitar named "Quiet Dignity" smashing through a glass window. One by one, the various pieces of our new musical venture were coming together. But we still had yet to find a breakthrough performance opportunity.

A few weeks later I was assigned to the far end of the island and was working in an area that knew very little about Mormons. The traditional methods of street contacting were, of course, very ineffective, and the people there were generally suspicious of outside religions. They didn't think too highly of foreigners like us trying to worm our way into their neighborhoods. So we spent most of our time trying to integrate with the community in innovative ways and show them that we were just ordinary, good-natured fellow humans, hoping to find that effectual door the mission president had promised us. One night we stumbled through it quite by accident.

The town doctor had befriended other missionaries several months before, so we kept in contact with her and tried to remain on friendly terms. One night she invited us to stop by her house for a chat. As we were sitting on the porch with her husband, telling them about our lives in America and answering questions as to why we had volunteered for our missions, a car pulled up and a new visitor walked to the door. The doctor was instantly chagrined as she remembered that she had also invited this friend for dinner that night, completely forgetting that we would be visiting as well. We offered to leave as she was clearly embarrassed about her mistake, but she graciously welcomed him in, insisted we stay, and invited him to join us and introduced us as her Mormon missionary neighbors.

Imagine our surprise as this unexpected guest introduced himself as the director of an island musical festival that would be held in a few weeks. He was looking for new musical acts to showcase and wondered if we knew anybody that would like to perform. My companion and I looked at each other like "Is this for real?" Needless to say, we were thrilled to volunteer, and he was equally excited to have an American Christian pop-rock band join the lineup.

The concert weekend arrived and the whole missionary band came up with their roadie companions. We spent the morning canvassing neighborhoods with flyers, contacting friends, making new acquaintances, and inviting people to come to the show. That night we rocked our full set to a sport center packed full of hundreds of people from the town and outlying tribes. For many people, it was their first time meeting a Mormon missionary, much less an American. We made a deep and lasting impression that weekend and were able to break down walls of superstition and ignorance in a wonderfully creative, musical way. We had finally found the effectual door.

You know, I don't really see much in the scriptures about bands or music or miracles like this, but there are other parallels and parables that fit the scenario pretty well. You could probably easily name three or four stories about vineyards and laborers striving to bring in a bountiful harvest for their Master, right? In Jacob 5, for example, you'll find a familiar story of a man working in an olive orchard, laboring diligently to bring in a harvest for his master. As you study the symbolism there, it's very easy to focus on obvious steps to success, such as planting good seeds and tenderly watching the young growth, pruning and transplanting where necessary, digging up and fertilizing the soil, and then just patiently waiting for the fruit to grow. But often overlooked are the preparatory, tedious steps of labor such as clearing out the scrub brush, removing rocks, and digging out stumps in order to break the hard ground and prepare to sow seeds. Most times it felt like I was doing a whole lot of spiritual rock removal and not much fruit harvesting! But that was my job—that's the work that was there for me to do. I can't claim any direct baptisms that happened as a result of our little missionary rock concert that night, but I know quite a few people went home with a gentler perspective on Mormonism than they had before. Maybe, just maybe, at some future point they'd be willing to give another missionary a chance, now that their heart had been softened a bit.

Sometimes people's hearts may take years of preparation before they are ready to accept seeds of faith and goodwill. Heck, even Brigham Young studied the Book of Mormon for a good two years before deciding to join Joseph Smith's church! So don't let frustration overcome you if you don't find easy success early on. When you find yourself struggling to unlock the effectual door, don't give up or give in to discouragement. The walls around their hearts may seem impregnable, and layers of generational superstitions may seem impossible to dig out. But keep your faith centered in He who led you there in the first place, and keep working to find your answer. Just like the Israelite armies in the days of Joshua, you too may need to circle your own "walls of Jericho" a magical seven times before they come crumbling down, but crumble they will, revealing the heart-door of those who are finally humble enough to receive Him by receiving you. When your hard work is paired with humble obedience and offered to God with faithful patience, you may qualify for the divine marvels of He who sent you on His errand. His timing can't be rushed or dictated, and your obedience can't be faked for counterfeited. But when both come together, wonderful things can happen.

As Ezra Taft Benson once said, "When obedience ceases to be an irritant and becomes our quest, in that moment God will endow us with power."[14]

UNLOCKED BY PATIENT OBEDIENCE

Our final concert of the season was going to be held at Easter time. We planned to host an outdoor festival showcasing a dozen musical numbers, performances by choirs, soloists, and ensembles, and video projections of inspirational images and religious art on a large screen above the performance area. Members from all across the island would be caravanning with friends and family to come for this performance, so the pressure was on to put on a fantastic production.

Of course, when the expectations are high, that's usually a cue to the universe for everything to go *wrong*.

We had spent several weeks writing a script, memorizing lines, practicing our performances, testing the audio and lighting gear, and working with our congregations to publicize the event. We set up a stage on the outdoor basketball court of our chapel, wired up the donated sound system, and strung hundreds of strands of lights through all the palm trees. Branch members had invited their non-member friends and families to attend, and we had several dozen investigators that had committed to show up as well. Everything was going according to plan and shaping up to be a wonderful success.

Everything, of course, except for the weather.

You know, you would think that after living on a tropical island for a year, I would have gotten accustomed to unexpected cloudbursts and would have been prepared for just about anything. But, man, I was still surprised at just how much water could unexpectedly dump from the skies. This wasn't just the "windows of heaven" opening up—this was more like the "neighbors in heaven left their sprinklers on overnight and flooded the dang yard!"

The morning of our concert I stood in the doorway of the chapel, looking over our soaked performance stage and soggy sets, feeling hopeless and defeated. "Come on, elders! Let's stay positive, elders!" said a zone leader cheerfully as we watched the gutters overflow and gush into the parking lot. I wondered if he was looking at the same rainstorm I was. "Maybe it'll let up by lunchtime?" he persisted cheerfully. "I bet the members will still come with their friends. We just have to have faith that this will turn out okay!"

I don't need faith to get through this, I thought to myself as I watched the water rising up toward our doorstep. *I need a snorkel and a life jacket!*

But we stuck to our schedule and spent the day finishing our preparations, setting up the audience chairs, and erecting the rest of the set, drenched to the skin. It rained all day and into the afternoon without letting up.

It was now two hours before the show was supposed to go live, and the rains still were tumb-a-ling down (and the floods were about to come up!). The rest of the elders and sisters had arrived from across the island, wondering whether all our preparations would be washed away in the storm.

One hour to go, and a few members had arrived at the chapel. They looked at our sets and gear, saw us huddling in chapel doorways, and wondered if they should stay for the show or not. A few of them shook their heads and drove off, disappointed. One family rolled up and asked if they could do anything to help. "Pray for the rain to stop!" we replied.

Thirty minutes until showtime. More cars were now starting to line

I don't need faith to get through this. . . . I need a snorkel and a life jacket!

up outside the chapel, but their passengers all stayed inside the cars, dry, doubtful, and disappointed. We appreciated their faith in our plans and willingness to support the show, but we could completely understand their misgivings about whether the show would go on.

"Okay elders, we've run out of time. There's only one thing left to do," our zone leader called out to us, finally sounding defeated as he waved us into the cultural hall. He had to half-yell to be heard over the relentless rain pounding on the chapel's metal roof. "We have one last chance to ask for a miracle."

We knelt down in a circle, alternating elders and sisters, and the zone leader led us in prayer, raising his voice so we could hear him over the rain. "Dear Lord, we need your help. We've tried to use our talents to share this gospel message and have done everything we could to put together tonight's presentation. We have tried our best to be obedient to the mission rules. We have tried our best to be patient in all our struggles. We've done all we can, Father . . . but we can't stop the rain. Please, wilt Thou do so? And if not, please bless us to be okay with that too."

He finished and we all stood and hugged each other, the guys patting each other on the back as if to say "good game, nice try." I sighed in frustration and got ready to galosh my way to the stage to start breaking the set down when I noticed something really strange.

The world had suddenly gone very, very quiet—like someone hit a big MUTE button in the sky.

My brain didn't quite register what had happened and I looked at my companion in bewilderment. "Do you hear that?" he asked, also confused. "It sounds like . . . like . . . *silence!*" I caught my breath as we ran outside. The trees were still dripping, the chairs and sets were all wet and puddled, but everything was silent and still. I looked up to the sky.

A hole had opened in the clouds directly above our chapel, just big enough to stop the rain over the church grounds. Across the street and all around us the rain continued to fall, but our little corner of Zion was enveloped in a bubble of warm, calm air.

Our prayers had been answered.

The members who had stayed were getting out of their cars, looking at the sky in amazement, while more and more cars drove up.

The investigators had kept their word too and were arriving just as the rain stopped, all full of smiles and ready to see the performance. "Wow, elders, how did you make that happen?" they laughed as they pointed to the sky. We shrugged and laughed as we ran to clean up the sets. In no time we had shaken out all the chairs, wiped down the sets, verified the lights and sound gear were all still working, and thrown open the gates.

The performance went off beautifully without a hitch. The members loved it, the investigators were deeply moved, and many families approached us after the show, requesting more information and wondering how they could be taught by us. One family even pulled me aside and said their aunt had visited that night, and by the time of the closing musical number she had received the testimony she needed that this was God's Church and she wanted to join. It turned out to be fantastic evening all around.

Once the show was over, everyone pitched in to tear down the set and dismantle the lighting and sound gear. Just as we started taking down the rest of the chairs and the lights, the sky-hole closed and the clouds filled in again above us. The rain resumed just where it had left off, drenching everything around us.

This time I didn't mind so much getting soaked. I smiled to the sky, arms open as I soaked up the rain and offered what must have been my five-hundredth prayer of thanksgiving that night, for now I truly knew for myself:

Miracles happen, and they're unlocked by patient obedience.

I, the Lord, am bound when ye do what I say; but when ye do not what I say, ye have no promise.

–D&C 82:10

TRUTH #4

Timing Is Everything, and It's in God's Hands

My life is but a weaving
Between my God and me.
I cannot choose the colors
He weaveth steadily.

Oft' times He weaveth sorrow;
And I in foolish pride
Forget He sees the upper
And I the underside.

Not 'til the loom is silent
And the shuttles cease to fly
Will God unroll the canvas
And reveal the reason why.

The dark threads are as needful
In the weaver's skillful hand
As the threads of gold and silver
In the pattern He has planned

He knows, He loves, He cares;
Nothing this truth can dim.
He gives the very best to those
Who leave the choice to Him.

—Author unknown

EVEN UNTIL THE LAST

There's a story in the Book of Mormon about a couple of missionaries who were bound up and thrown in prison by a wicked crowd, only to be delivered later when the prison walls came tumbling down. My Sunday School teachers would recite the story as an example of how God would protect His servants. I saw the story a little bit differently, though—it's an example of how often God will make them wait, suffer, and trust in His timing.

As the story goes, the people of Ammonihah had quite a reputation for scumbaggery, especially the lawyers. (*I know, I know, big surprise, right? It's* always *the lawyers.*) One thing's for sure—wherever there are people in need of repentance, God will send servants to help them remember Him, even if they must speak harsh truths. In this case, God sent Alma and Amulek to try and reclaim the people of Ammonihah, and boy, did they have a rough time of it from the start. When the prominent lawyer Zeezrom tried to bribe them to deny their testimonies and renounce God in front of the public, Alma doubled down on his testimony and taught one of the most sublime sermons on the plan of salvation ever recorded.

A few people listening that day were converted, but the majority of the crowd kept their ears closed and hearts hardened. They snatched up the missionaries, roughed them up, and threw them in jail, leaving them to rot. The people who had converted were martyred in flames while Alma and Amulek were forced to watch, the people's screams penetrating their already broken hearts. Day after day the two men starved in jail, the monotony broken up only by their jailers coming in to beat and torture them. Still the two men held on to their faith, trusting that God was aware of their plight.

And they waited and waited and waited. Despite their pleas and prayers and desperation, the heavens remained as closed as their jail cell doors.

Finally after "many days" (Alma 14:23), the regular crowd of lawyers and judges showed up once again to deliver a beatdown on the helpless prisoners. But this time, the scriptures tell us that it turned out differently:

And the chief judge stood before them, and smote them again, and said unto them: If ye have the power of God deliver yourselves from these bands, and then we will believe that the Lord will destroy this people according to your words.

And it came to pass that they all went forth and smote them, saying the same words, *even until the last*; and when the last had spoken unto them the power of God was upon Alma and Amulek, and they rose and stood upon their feet.

And Alma cried, saying: How long shall we suffer these great afflictions, O Lord? O Lord, give us strength according to our faith which is in Christ, even unto deliverance. And they broke the cords with which they were bound. (Alma 14:24–26, emphasis added)

Every time I read that story, I can't help but wonder: did God really have to wait until the last guy got his hits in? Couldn't He have intervened before the *first* attack instead of the last? Couldn't he have prevented the whole thing from happening? Can't you imagine Alma and Amulek looking at the lawyers all lined up waiting to take their turn whacking

Truth #4: Timing is everything.

the "Missionary Piñata" and wondering, *Any time now, God! There's quite a crowd queued up today, and it looks like they brought Bruiser von Ironfist, Esquire to play! A little help here, please?*

But it wasn't to be. Like Joseph Smith in Liberty Jail, like Abinadi before King Noah, and even like our Savior in the Garden of Gethsemane, there was a reason—unknown to them—why God let them wait it out. It wasn't up to them to decide when help would come, or in what form. All they could do was to trust in God and in His timetable.

We won't always be able to see the end of our trials from the beginning nor understand the full pattern that God has sketched out—which He unfolds for us one piece at a time. We may be frustrated as we watch life's seasons pass us by while our wishes remain unfulfilled, the bud of our heart's desires left closed on the tree. But if our faith is grounded firm in He who moves the heavens, we will eventually see the glorious blossom of not just what we *desired*, but what we truly *needed*. God does hear and answer prayers, and many times what we think is a "No" is actually a "Not yet, child. Just you wait. Trust me—this is gonna be good."

Truth #4: Timing is everything.

ONE WHITE ROBE LEADS TO ANOTHER

A new elder showed up at the missionary office one day, hailing from the exotic, faraway land of Pocatello, Idaho. At this time we were thick in the middle of our Christmas singing tour, so naturally we asked him if he had any musical talent or other skills he could share. "Uh, nope, can't even sing," he sheepishly replied. "But I *am* a black belt in karate. Shotokan-style."

Yeah, we didn't believe him either. But a quick demonstration of a technique called "almost kicking my companion in the face when he wouldn't stop teasing me" showed that this elder was serious business. There's something about knowing your companion could take you down in a heartbeat that kinda makes you respect the guy, you know? (Couldn't I have had someone like him when I was back in Lifou? I wondered. Bring on the mobs, baby, I've got my own personal Batman!)

As he watched the rest of us going about our musical performances, Elder Phillips thought that maybe he could use his martial arts talents somehow, so he wrote home and asked for his parents to ship him his karate *gi* and belt. He knew the boats would be slow and it would take several months for the gear to arrive, so in the meantime we went about our work, focusing on sharing the gospel message in whatever traditional way we could.

A few months later the mission president called him in to the office and told him that he and his companion would be transferred out on a special assignment. They were going north to a tiny town called Koumac and would officially open the city to the preaching of the gospel. The town had exactly two known LDS members, and the nearest branch was a 2½-hour bus ride away. The missionaries were to establish a presence in the town, get to know the locals, and "break up the ground" in preparation for the seeds of the gospel to be planted. The mission office had already procured an apartment for them to use as a home base and the members had been notified of the incoming elders, but still it would be difficult, isolated, and lonely work.

The elders squared their shoulders and courageously rose to the challenge that awaited them far away from the rest of us. By now, Elder Phillips's karate *gi* had finally arrived from home, so he took that with him, just in case.

On the first day they arrived in Koumac, they spent some time driving through the town, getting to know the various shopkeepers, schoolmasters, and locals that had established a city in such a remote area. The town had the usual sort of businesses, churches, small motels, and a regional boarding school—and a gym that caught Elder Phillips's eye as they drove past one day. He excitedly yelled at his companion to stop the car.

Above the gym was a sign for Shotokan Karate. They had found the only dojo around for two hundred miles.

They introduced themselves to the sensei and quickly became friends. They learned that he taught both youth and adult classes in karate and kickboxing and invited the Americans to join, if they were interested. One quick phone call to the mission president later, and faster than you can say "sweep the leg, Johnny!" the missionaries were dressed in workout clothes and had joined the class. Soon they discovered that being in the class was a great way to introduce themselves to the community, since they chatted with the kids' parents before and after class and got to know the teens that would come for sparring practice. (Plus the local kids got a kick out of being able to beat up on the Americans, all in the name of "exercise." I was "volunteered" to be the punching bag on more than one occasion.) The elders were even invited to judge a regional karate tournament and were featured in the local newspaper as the guest judges from America.

Elder Phillips's karate skills continued to be an effective door-opener to the people of Koumac. When a new couple moved in to the town and introduced themselves as national Judo/Jiu-Jitsu champions, they received a warm welcome at the dojo and joined the missionaries' circle of friends. Soon the elders were training martial arts for 4 hours a day, 3 days a week as part of their "Finding Activities" and organizing service projects to advertise their classes.

When the elders had initially traveled to the outlying villages around Koumac, they were greeted with cold disinterest and suspicion. But word and reputation both travel quickly in small villages like this, and many of the kids that had sparred with the elders in class had now gone home to their tribes and told their parents about how cool the Americans were. So when the elders returned to their tribes a few months later, offering free karate and English language classes for the village kids, they got sign-ups by the dozens and were warmly welcomed as guests, strangers no more. Slowly and surely the fruits of kindness, trust, and charity spread throughout the land.

The karate sensei, François, and his wife, Eveline, were originally uninterested in the message of the restored gospel. But day by day their relationship of trust grew, one karate class at a time, (and frequently over friendly games of chess at François's house after class) until finally they said they were willing to listen to the message Elder Phillips had come to share. The timing was now right, the season had come, and the ground that had taken so long to break open was at last ready to receive the seeds of faith.

They listened. They felt the Spirit. They were invited to act on it. And they committed.

Elder Phillips traded his white karate *gi* for a white shirt, tie, and slacks, and he walked with François and Evelyn into the ocean waters of baptism several weeks later.

THE PATH TO THE GREAT CHIEF

Wouldn't it be wonderful if every time we faced a trial or a challenge, we could know exactly how long it would last and when it would be over? I've wished for this myself and my loved ones *so* many times, since I've struggled to have faith that God's timing will work out for our good. Sometimes we just have to "let go and let God," holding on till the end when all is revealed and made right. That's how our faith grows, step by unseeing step, trial by seemingly unending trial. But when our faith is grounded upon the knowledge that God loves us and is guiding our path, we can remain confident that our choices are leading us onward and upward. The road we follow is difficult, sure, but it is the *right* road.

Let me tell you a story about another man we met, whose life path took him to a surprising place. His name is Samuel, and he lived in a hut in a neighboring tribe in Lifou.

First a bit of background: the island of Lifou is divided into three kingdoms, each ruled by a great chief. Within each kingdom are eight tribes, each governed by a chief and council of elders. The traditional Lifou dwellings are grass huts designed symbolically around this tribal organization: a large center support trunk, representing the great chief, bears

The road we follow is difficult, sure, but it is the *right* road.

most of the weight and sits in the middle of the floor. Smaller poles, representing the lesser chiefs and elders, encircle it and support the walls and ceiling. Branches and woven grass on the roof represent the tribe members, working together to keep the hut strong, safe, and secure. The door of each hut is built low to the ground, requiring one to bow to the great chief as they enter. Well-constructed huts, like well-constructed tribes, last for multiple generations and are even capable of withstanding a full-strength hurricane. (Not even the imported French military buildings could make that claim!)

Several years before I arrived on the island, the missionaries had worked with the Aliki family and the great chief of our southern kingdom to gain permission to move freely about and teach the gospel to anyone interested. The north kingdom, however, was off-limits to proselyting. We could visit them but not openly teach, on penalty of expulsion (or worse . . .). The members had struggled and prayed for a way to officially get in contact with the great chief in the north and officially open up that area, but so far nothing had worked. (The middle kingdom had already denied our requests.)

The biggest obstacle was the tradition of exclusivity for the great chief—the general public wasn't allowed to speak to him, and only certain select clan members could even visit his palace grounds. Every clan in the tribe had a different job: some were cooks, others were security, and they even had a clan assigned to swoosh away mosquitoes and flies from the great chief's face.

One day a young woman in our tribe asked us if we'd talk to her boyfriend, a local DJ named Samuel. She wasn't interested in God or the gospel, but *he* was, on account of having (*you guessed it*) a vision. He wanted to know why God would appear to him and tell him to clean up his life and learn more about heaven, but why none of his tribe's pastors would believe his story. (I couldn't believe it either as his girlfriend told us his backstory. What *was* it with the people there having visions all the time?)

Our initial visit with Samuel was very straightforward. He was a party-hard kind of guy with long dreadlocks, a big friendly smile, and a quiet voice. His DJ lifestyle took him all over the island where he threw big parties full of drugs, booze, and kava (a traditional narcotic drink that had recently been added to the Word of Wisdom for Pacific Islanders). He was successful in what he did and happy with his life, but he couldn't deny the vision he'd had or the feeling that he could become something *better*. So we gave him a copy of the Book of Mormon, told him about Joseph Smith, invited him to read and pray about it, and set a date for our next visit. That was the last time I saw him. Or I should say, the *old* him.

Because on the day of our next appointment, he had completely changed. His dreadlocks were shorn, he had been completely sober for several days, and he had thrown all his marijuana, alcohol, and kava into the ocean. "Um, Samuel, did someone tell you about the Mormon Word of Wisdom already?" I asked, astonished at his newly radiating countenance.

"The word of what? I don't know what you're talking about, brother," he replied, smiling. "I just thought that if I'm going to truly follow God now, I should clean up right. All that stuff I used to do . . . it's bad for me. I need to just start fresh with a new life. I want that old life behind me."

He was baptized two weeks later.

But that was only the beginning of his story.

One day after our little branch sacrament meeting, he approached my companion and I as we said good-bye to our members and watched them pad off through the jungle trails back to their huts. He asked if we'd ever thought about going into the northern kingdoms to teach people. "Oh sure, Samuel," we answered. "But we can't get there until the chief invites us. Not gonna happen."

"Well, I think I can get you in," he replied. "I don't know if I told you, but I'm from the north kingdom. My family is part of the spokesperson clan. We're kind of special—we're the only ones allowed to bring in strangers from the outside."

(Yeah, my jaw was pretty much hitting the jungle floor by now.)

He continued. "I haven't really spoken with the chief's family in a long time and I don't know if he'll remember me. The best I can do is send them a message that I'd like to come visit, and then we'll have to trust God to open the path for us. We'll drop in unannounced, visit the palace, and ask to talk to the chief and introduce you guys to him."

I couldn't believe how this was unfolding! We decided on a date and fasted all the day and night before, pleading to God to open a way for us to teach the gospel to His children. The next morning we set off for the north kingdom, bearing the offering of *coutume* with a gift of money, tribal cloth, a picture of Jesus Christ, and a French Book of Mormon to present to the great chief. Samuel was nervous as we drove, fiddling with his tie and new white shirt, trying to remember everything we should or shouldn't do if we were able to gain access. "Just let me do most of the talking," he said. "I'll have a lot to say in our language, and then if he looks at you and allows it, you can talk." He was jittery from excitement and a little scared about what could happen if things went wrong and guided us as we drove along the single-track roads.

"Oh wait, turn right here!" he said, motioning to a dirt road leading off the main road. We would have driven right passed a hidden opening in the jungle had Samuel not pointed it out to us. Tree branches reached out onto the trail on both sides, scraping the car as we slowly drove forward. It was evident nobody had traveled this way for a long time. "This is the customary trail for my clan to use to approach the great chief's hut," Samuel explained. "Only the closest families are allowed to come this way."

We arrived at a large clearing rimmed by walls made of stacked lava rock and parked the car. At the clearing's edges, tucked into the coconut trees, were a handful of smaller huts with closed doors. No one was visible. "Those are the bodyguard clans," Samuel said quietly, pointing to the small huts. "In the old days, that clan would just kill any trespassing stranger on sight. But I think they've mostly stopped doing that." (Mostly *stopped?* I thought. *Dude, how about* all *stopped?*) We offered another prayer and stepped onto the grounds. No one stirred.

Samuel led us toward the giant chief hut sprawling at the clearing center. It was about six times the size of the huts we lived in and had been erected many years ago by the council of elders and all the supporting chiefs. Once upon a time the great chief lived inside it and held court, but now he used the comfortable French villa next door. We arrived outside, where Samuel motioned for us to stop.

"You know, I think you guys are the first white missionaries to step on these grounds in over one hundred years. Let's hope the chief is feeling happy today."

He called out to the villa in his native tongue, opened the doors, and walked in. We saw him disappear around the corner and heard voices of someone approaching him, speaking softly.

My companion and I stood there for what felt like an eternity. I tried to mask my nervousness, praying that the chief would welcome us, and passed the time by counting mosquitoes I slapped away. (They sure loved the taste of pasty Utah flesh!) I was almost up to thirty when Samuel appeared again at the doorway with a big smile on his face. He gestured for us to follow him and turned back in to the villa.

We entered a lavishly decorated living room decorated with oversized masks, tapa cloth tapestries, and even an enormous whale jawbone resting in a corner. Samuel presented us to the great chief's wife, who welcomed us politely, and the great chief himself, a greying grizzled hulk of a man. He shook our hands but didn't say anything, clearly curious about these young foreign visitors.

Samuel performed his ceremonial greeting and spoke for a long time, while the great chief responded in short grunts and glances at us. Finally Samuel motioned for us to present our gifts.

My companion took the lead. "Sir, we have come from America to live among your people. We are here as servants of Jesus Christ, and we bear a message of love, service, kindness, and revelation from God. We have been living in the south kingdom for some time now, and with your blessing and permission, would like to teach the people of your lands as well. We respect your laws and traditions and only wish to serve God's children here, if you will grant us leave to do so."

The great chief sat in thought for a minute and looked at his wife as if to gauge her reaction. Then he quietly nodded his head and smiled. He spoke to us in French, telling us that we would still need to visit the lesser chiefs of each tribe individually, but that we could tell them he was on our side and we should have free reign.

I heaved a sigh of relief and offered a silent prayer of gratitude. We thanked him. Samuel stood at the side, beaming with pride at having made this all possible. The doors that had been closed for so long had finally been opened, once the timing was just right.

God had spoken to a humble, ordinary man—a drug-dealing party DJ—and called him to live a higher life and be a light in the darkness for his fellow natives. We had finally found the right path to the great chief of the northern kingdom.

HARVESTING WHAT OTHERS HAVE PLANTED

Waiting on God's timetable can often be a frustrating endeavor, especially because each person's specific tasks as a missionary will be very unique. There is no "one size fits all" role in the gospel. While you may be looking forward to harvesting the many souls who are ready to join God's Church, you may instead find yourself struggling just to break ground or pull out the stubborn stumps and rocks of people's hearts. Sometimes you'll need to help prune incorrect faith traditions, or spend extra time nourishing budding shoots of testimony that seem to grow in slow motion. Perhaps if you're lucky, you'll have chances to easily sow seeds of truth in plowed heart-fields ready to receive, teaching families that just seem perfectly prepared for the gospel. More than once you'll probably be asked to put up with what feels like a lot of useless bull crap (which just may be a nourishing fertilizer inconveniently packaged as animal dung). It's no fun to have to spread that around and get caught in it, but deep down we know that it's actually good for us. And every once in a while the timing may be just right for you to bring in the harvest so carefully watched over and tended by others.

Regardless of which role you have to play in God's vineyard, you need to trust that He knows the seasons of the heart for every person on earth and will give them what they need, when they need it. Your labor then is to serve in any capacity and trust that the Master of the vineyard knows best what is needed.

He knows the seasons of the heart for every person on earth.

Consider this story from *Preach My Gospel* of a sister missionary who was called to serve in the same area where her older sibling had worked. The timing wasn't right when the first sister was there, but things had certainly changed by the time the second sister came around:

> Much to my surprise, I was called to labor in the same mission where my older sister had served a year earlier. After a few months in the mission field, I was transferred to one of the areas where my sister had served. Upon learning of my transfer, my sister wrote and asked me to visit a family that she and her companion had taught. She expressed the love and closeness she had with the Norman family and how disappointed she was when they discontinued investigating the Church.
>
> My companion and I located the Normans and were warmly received by them. They accepted our invitation to again hear the restored gospel. I'm not sure what the difference was this time, but they were fully ready to accept our message. The entire family was baptized and confirmed.
>
> After this experience, I wondered about other former investigators my sister had worked with. I thought, "If it worked for the Normans, maybe it will work for other people she taught as well." I decided to write my sister about the idea of contacting other people she had taught. She went through her journal and sent me the names of other former investigators in the area.
>
> My companion and I spent the next week contacting these people. To our delight, almost half of them accepted an invitation to hear the restored gospel again. Several of this group were baptized and confirmed. While meeting with these former investigators, we also asked them for referrals of their friends and acquaintances that would be interested in our message. As a result, we found additional people to teach. This was the busiest time of my mission.[15]

Not every fruit ripens at the same time. If you try to harvest it too soon or fertilize it too much, it will die. So don't try to teach people faster than they are ready to receive or move them through the conversion process according to your time line. In your zeal to see "progress," don't get caught up in setting dates and goals on their behalf—let them set a date for themselves and make their own commitments. Invite them to take action according to the whisperings of the Spirit in their hearts, but let them grow in their own way and at their own speed. Those investigators who take their time to be genuine in their gospel study may not progress as quickly as you prefer, but it is their journey to take. You're just the Sherpa helping them along the way, whatever their pace may be.

ACCEPTING YOUR OWN TIMETABLE

Being patient with God's timing also includes His timing for you.

There is a possibility that you may not be ready to go on a mission when you turn eighteen.

Or nineteen.

Or even into your twenties.

And that's okay.

On the day that the new age for mission eligibility was announced, Church leaders held a press conference to explain the details of the change and answer questions from the media. Several concerns were voiced that the age change would be considered the new *requirement*, that kids would feel they *had* to turn in their papers the moment they turned eighteen. And such worries are reasonable—there's a lot of pressure in our Mormon culture to serve missions. Unfortunately, such pressure, while well-intentioned and often meant to be constructive, can sometimes lead young people out on missions for the wrong reasons.

I've known people who served missions primarily out of fear of disappointing others or because they were expected to do so by parents or grandparents. Some may put in their mission papers because they want to avoid embarrassing questions from nosy ward members as to why they haven't left yet. I've even known guys who served because their parents promised them rewards when they got home, like a new car or college tuition. And I'm sure there is more than one person out there who served a mission because a girlfriend or boyfriend said they only wanted to marry an RM.

In each of these experiences, the person was motivated by the pressures of guilt or duty, rather than genuine conversion and a desire to share the gospel. Such pressures are the unfortunate reality of our culture. Perhaps we could gently correct this by recalling the words of Elder Russel M. Nelson on the day of the press conference: "No young man or woman should begin his or her service as a missionary *before they are ready*. . . . Church leaders are emphasizing that the change does not suggest that all missionaries should or will serve at an earlier age than before. The change simply provides an option for young people to begin their missionary service earlier, if they are prepared to do so."[16]

Being ready to serve is a *big deal*, requires a lot of work, and is not something that can be rushed or counterfeited. Preparing to invest eighteen to twenty-four months of your life in missionary endeavors will require a lot of emotional and psychological growth, and those who want to do so will each reach their "ready" state at a different pace—there is no one universal best time for everyone. In fact, some of the best missionaries I ever met were those who, for one reason or another, served later than they were expected to. Such varsity missionaries were frequently wiser, calmer, more confident, and harder working than us sophomore guys. So please don't worry about going on a mission "late" if you're not feeling ready when you're eighteen or nineteen. To paraphrase the wizard Gandalf the Grey, "A new missionary is never 'late,' nor is he early. He arrives precisely when God wants him to." You shouldn't go on a mission just because you're *supposed* to, but because you *want* to and are *ready* to.

As the Lord said to Joseph Smith, "Sanctify yourselves that your minds become single to God, and the days will come that you shall see him; for he will unveil his face unto you, and *it shall be in his own time*, and in his own way, and according to his own will" (D&C 88:68; emphasis added).

IT'S IN GOD'S HANDS

Just as we are not to judge when people are supposed to join the Church or leave on a mission, neither should we judge harshly those young people whose missions take different forms, nor those who choose not to go at all. Some may be invited to serve as Church-service missionaries, welfare missionaries, short-term local missionaries, or in any other number of honorable, faithful ways. And many decide that, for their own reasons, a mission just isn't for them, but they still decide to be an active, vibrant, and contributory member of the Church. God loves them no less, because serving a mission isn't a litmus test of personal righteousness. Our duty as fellow Saints is to have nothing but loving kindness and charity toward them.

And toward yourself, especially if you're wanting to serve but currently are not worthy to do so. It is so easy to get down on yourself and feel that you're somehow less of a human because of mistakes you've made. If you need to get things straightened out with your bishop, *that's okay*. Think of him as a private coach that will help you use your preparatory time to fix those things that are out of place in your life, to strengthen what once was weak, and to help you stay on track with your training before you're ready to jump in to the big game of missionary work. If you are asked to wait for a bit before submitting your papers, it doesn't mean that God doesn't want you or that He's disappointed in your choices. It means He *does* want you to serve and He wants you to be at your absolute best and most prepared before you head out.

Make sure you counsel with the Lord often and honestly if you choose to go, and listen to what He tells you in your heart. Have the courage and humility to discuss your preparations openly with your parents and your bishop. Remember that being eligible to serve is merely a matter of age, but being prepared to serve is a matter of effort. So trust in God's timing for your own personal preparations. Don't compare yourself to those in your classes or quorums, for you are growing at a different rate than them.

God can change caterpillars into butterflies, sand into pearls, and coal into brilliant, precious diamonds using mostly just pressure and time. So if you feel like you're under a lot of pressure, maybe just give it more time.

Timing is everything, and it's in God's hands.

❧

The issue for us is trusting God enough to trust also His timing. If we can truly believe He has our welfare at heart, may we not let His plans unfold as He thinks best? The same is true with the second coming and with all those matters wherein our faith needs to include faith in the Lord's timing for us personally, not just in His overall plans and purposes.

—Neal A. Maxwell[17]

TRUTH #5

Love the People. There Is No Substitute

"It is a time-honored adage that love begets love. Let us pour forth love—show forth our kindness unto all mankind, and the Lord will reward us with everlasting increase; cast our bread upon the waters and we shall receive it after many days, increased to a hundredfold. Friendship is like Brother Turley in his blacksmith shop welding iron to iron; it unites the human family with its happy influence."

–Joseph Smith[18]

LESS IS MORE

When I was preparing to turn in my papers, I would frequently get caught up in the excitement of all the new stuff I'd get to buy. I spent countless hours at the various missionary supply stores in Utah County, walking the aisles of country-themed knickknacks, imagining which land I'd be called to and planning out all the clothes, tools, doodads, and other mostly useless junk I'd be bringing along. I pictured my home covered in flags and maps and photo boards of all my adventures. There may have been a cross-stitched missionary quote in there somewhere. The day I arrived at the MTC, I was staggering like a pack mule on Kilimanjaro as I lugged my suitcases to the drop-off point.

Many weeks later, when I finally arrived in the islands, I found out I didn't need any of it.

"Elder, we're going out to live with a family in the jungle. All you need is a couple sets of clothes and your scriptures," my new senior companion told me. We were hanging out with other elders in the mission office on a cool breezy night. The next morning he and I would be boarding a catamaran and sailing out to Lifou for my first trip.

"But . . . but . . . what about this gold-plated nail grooming set and shoe polishing kit? My wind-up alarm clock and radio? The embroidered handkerchiefs? My travel-sized bottle of CK *Obsession*? Can't I bring those too? I mean, we want to look *nice*, don't we?" I asked, fearfully clutching my bags of junk. I'd worked hard to earn money to buy it, and there was no way I was just going to dump it all in the mission office and leave it behind.

"Elder, you have to understand something about these people," my companion patiently answered. "You're going to see families of ten to fifteen people living together in a one-room hut. Most of them don't have shoes, let alone multiple sets of clothes. Half of the tribes don't have running water, and most don't even have electricity. All your extra gear is just going to get in the way and make you look like an outsider even more than you already do. We've found that we do best if we live like they do—as simply as we can. In fact, maybe you should go read Alma 17 through 24 tonight. That pretty much sums up how we do missionary work out there."

So that night I studied the story of Ammon and the Lamanites, and I started to see his experiences in a truly different light. Ammon came from a wealthy, royal family and could have had a life of luxury and peace had he stayed home and taken his place on the throne. But instead he set it all aside, traveled to a far-off country at great risk to his own safety, and, finding himself captured and interrogated, humbly stated that he simply wanted to live with them and serve them.

Such a thing had likely never been seen before by the Lamanites, let alone in the royal household. A real Nephite prince, there to be a servant? Ammon's disarming personality must have scored some big points with the Lamanite court, since they tried to hook him up with the king's daughter. (Strategic alliance to a rival princess, maybe?) But to his credit, Ammon refused and insisted that he was just there to serve and work, even if it meant mucking out stables and sleeping outdoors with the flocks. His intent was genuine—he was there to dwell among the people, as he said, even "until the day [he] die[d]" (Alma 17:23).

So that's what we tried to do too. We lived in the huts with our host family, slept on the same floor mats, joined in the cooking rotation and chore duty. We received permission to use our missionary car to shuttle people around the tribe, so we'd get up at dawn with them and go working in their fields, even in our white shirts and ties sometimes. When the branch boys invited us to go camping in a seaside cliff one weekend, we took along some investigators and made it a Young Men activity. We did our best to learn their tribal dialect, learn their songs and dances, and participate in their customs. I learned what it meant to become *genuine* friends with the people, regardless of whether or not they were interested in the gospel. We celebrated in their weddings, rejoiced over babies born, and mourned over those unexpectedly lost. We rebuilt with them after storms ravaged villages, hosted FHEs, served on city committees and councils, taught early morning seminary, gave musical numbers at special events and firesides, learned how to repair their vehicles, dedicated graves, counseled those who had strayed, blessed those who were sick, and sometimes just sat and listened to those who needed a sympathetic ear.

And my companion was right about all the gear I'd brought along: I didn't need any of it. (I actually wound up giving most of it away.) At first I was shocked at how few personal belongings the

Truth #5: Love the people. natives had, yet how happy they were—and I realized that they understood a simple truth of life. When it came to teaching the gospel, I found that *less* could actually be *more*. The less stuff I had with me, the less I had to worry about and the more I could devote myself fully to serving and loving the people.

And that was really the key to finding true missionary success: a genuine, charitable, self-sacrificing desire for everyone around us to have their absolute best life. That kind of love doesn't come easy for some people. Heck, even the scriptures say we need to pray with "all the energy of heart" in order to be filled with it (Moroni 7:48). For me, the transformation into a true charitable missionary would only come over time as I gradually became refined and polished and learned how to love them as Christ did.

Truth #5: Love the people.

THE MARKS OF A MAN

The great thing about developing that level of charity is that you can't help but be changed as you acquire it. (Perhaps such transformation is *necessary* in order to achieve it?) Either way, when you begin to feel that kind of love for others, it leaves its mark on you. You'll never be the same person again. You gradually become a better, more polished version of yourself, usually in ways that you could never foresee. That polishing process reveals a mature, well-functioning version of ourselves that we may be surprised to find existed!

There's a story frequently circulated in the Church that describes this type of celestial refinement. It's usually attributed to David Bryan Wiser.

Marks Of A Man

"As I jumped on board my flight from Miami to Salt Lake City, I paused for a moment to catch my breath. Seated near the front of the plane was an excited young man, probably 19, sitting with his parents. His hair was short and his clothes new and sharp. His suit was fitted perfectly and his black shoes still retained that store bought shine. His body was in good shape, his face clear, and his hands clean. In his eyes I could see a nervous look, and his movements were that of an actor on opening night.

"He was obviously flying to Utah to become a missionary for the Mormon Church. I smiled as I walked by and took pride in belonging to this same Church where these young men and women voluntarily serve the Savior for two years. With this special feeling, I continued to the back where my seat was located.

"As I sat in my seat, I looked to the right and to my surprise, saw another missionary sleeping in the window seat. His hair was also short, but that was the only similarity between the two. This one was obviously returning home, and I could tell at a glance what type of missionary he had been.

"The fact that he was already asleep told me a lot. His entire body seemed to let out a big sigh. It looked as if this was the first time in two years he had even slept, and I wouldn't be surprised if it was. As I looked at his face, I could see the heavy bags under his eyes, the chapped lips, and the scarred and sunburned face caused by the fierce Florida sun.

"His suit was tattered and worn. A few of the seams were coming apart, and I noticed that there were a couple of tears that had been hand-sewn with a very sloppy stitch.

"I saw the nametag, crooked, scratched and bearing the name of the Church he represented, the engraving of which was almost all worn away. I saw the knee of his pants, worn and white, the result of many hours of humble prayer.

"A tear came to my eye as I saw the things that really told me what kind of missionary he had been. I saw the marks that made this boy a man. His feet—the two that had carried him from house to house, now lay there swollen and tired. They were covered by a pair of worn-out shoes. Many of the large scrapes and gouges had been filled in by the countless number of polishings.

"His books—laying across his lap were his scriptures, the word of God. Once new, these books which testify of Jesus Christ and His mission, were now torn, bent, and ragged from use.

"His hands—those big, strong hands, which had been used to bless and teach, were now scarred and cut from knocking at doors.

"Those were indeed the marks of that man. And as I looked at him, I saw the marks of another man, the Savior, as he was hanging on the cross for the sins of the world.

"His feet—those that had once carried him throughout the land during his ministry, were now nailed to the cross.

"His side—now pierced with a spear. Sealing his gospel, his testimony with his life.

"His hands—the hands that had been used to ordain his servants and bless the sick were also scarred with the nails that were pounded to hang him on the cross.

"Those were the marks of that Great Man.

"As my mind returned to the missionary, my whole body seemed to swell with pride and joy, because I knew, by looking at him, that he had served his Master well.

"My joy was so great, I felt like running to the front of the plane, grabbing that new, young missionary, and bringing him back to see what he can become, what he can do.

"But would he see the things that I saw, could anyone see the things I saw? Or would he just see the outward appearance of that mighty elder, tired and worn out, almost dead.

"As we landed, I reached over and tapped him to wake him up. As he awoke, it seemed like new life was entering his body. His whole frame just seemed to fill as he stood up, tall and proud. As he turned his face toward mine, I saw a light about his face that I had never seen before. I looked into his eyes. Those eyes, I will never forget those eyes. They were the eyes of a prophet, a leader, a follower, and a servant. They were the eyes of the Savior. No words were spoken. No words were needed.

"As we unloaded, I stepped aside to let him go first. I watched as he walked, slow but steady, tired but strong. I followed him and found myself walking the way that he did. When I came through the doors, I saw this young man in the arms of his parents, and I couldn't hold it any longer.

"With tears streaming down my face, I watched these loving parents greet their son who had been away for a short time. And I wondered if our parents in Heaven would greet us the same way. Will they wrap their arms around us and welcome us home from our journey on earth? I believe they will. I just hope that I can be worthy enough to receive such praise, as I'm sure this missionary will.

"I said a silent prayer, thanking the Lord for missionaries like this young man. I don't think I will ever forget the joy and happiness he brought me that day."

ADULTING FOR REAL

This polishing, refining, and maturing experience of missionary life can begin long before you get your call. I've often found that the people who had the most Christlike love for others were also the ones who had it all together in life. They were *mature*, in the best sense of the word. Their very character was refined and was revealed in all aspects of their well-functioning life. It's like they knew *how* to be an adult, and with that knowledge came the ability to show deeper, more genuine love for others.

Does this mean that you can't love others until your own life is in order? Of course not. But if God's house is a house of order (see D&C 132:8), we can safely believe that living a refined, orderly life can bring the Spirit of Christ into our hearts, and with it, greater love for those around us.

The good news is that this can totally be learned—"life hacks" to the rescue! If you're lucky, you may have been taught some of these tips and tricks by parents or leaders before your mission, but chances are you could still use a bit of coaching along the way. (As for me, I had only a tiny understanding of just how I was supposed to adult successfully before I was thrown out into the real world. Frankly, I'm surprised I didn't burn the hut down trying to cook dinner for myself.) Thankfully our mission president and his wife took it upon themselves to train us. Every couple of months they'd devote time to helping us learn how to be better versions of ourselves, with the goal of helping us become better vessels for Christ's love.

They showed up to zone conference one month with a special announcement. "Apparently we need to watch a movie with you, elders," the president said while the zone leaders wheeled out a TV on a cart and inserted a DVD. We were getting all excited—finally, something we're allowed to watch besides *Together Forever*! But our excitement was short-lived; the movie was about basic etiquette. "Manners for Missionaries," the title screen read. For reals. We all groaned and slumped in our seats. I think my senior companion punched me in the arm to wake me up.

The president chuckled but his eyes were stern as he looked at us. "I've had to watch this with our missionaries on the other islands, and based on the reports I've received from the senior couples who inspect your apartments, it sounds like you could use a few lessons as well."

So we sat there for an hour and learned Housekeeping 101. We laughed at the movie (while some of us secretly took notes. *Did you know that it's actually possible to properly fold a fitted sheet? Who knew, right?*) and promised the president we'd try our best to tidy up our flats. He assured us that the next inspections would be done in secret, and anyone who left a messy flat behind would lose their ceiling and floor fans for a month. (Oh, and none of the flats had air conditioning.)

Yeah, we sat up straight right away and committed to keep things clean.

At some point during the mission, something *clicked* for us. We realized that charity toward others and living in a Christlike way is really, really hard if your personal life is in shambles. I don't know about you, but I have a hard time imagining Christ giving the Sermon on the Mount and then walking home, collapsing onto a shabby sofa with empty takeout boxes scattered around Him on the floor. There's something about living as Christ would live that naturally requires maturity and refinement and becoming a better functioning adult.

So, with a desire to keep it 100 percent real, here is a quick run-down of some basic pointers every missionary should know in order to be a better, more loving version of yourself. You may already know most of these, and maybe this seems like so much common sense. But you'll find they're not all common *practice*.

Start Clean

"You simply can't be here with unresolved sins," said our MTC mission president on day one. "They will get in the way of your progress, impede revelation, and prevent you from being effective." The best thing you can do to make the MTC and mission life successful is to start with a clean slate. You can't fake being worthy. Have the courage and humility to counsel with your parents, bishop, and stake president to clear up mistakes from your past, even if it takes an uncomfortable amount of time. The longer you put it off, the harder it will be to face your past. So own up, (wo)man up, fess up, face up, clean up, move up, and move on.

Start Healthy

You'll likely be walking or riding a bike more during your mission than you had before, so don't put off your physical preparation.

BEN BERNARDS

If you've never done cardio exercise before, a good place to start would be to alternate walking and jogging in 2-minute intervals for a total duration of 30 minutes, three to four times a week. Try slowly increasing the jog interval and decreasing the walk interval until you can sustain a solid, steady jogging pace for a good 30–45 minutes at a time. "Starting healthy" also means facing up to other physical, mental, or emotional issues that may need resolution. Work with a professional to get whatever help you need before you begin your missionary service.

When you're in the MTC, eat just a little bit less than you want to. It will help prevent the typical MTC fifteen-pound weight gain and will help prepare you for the mission field, where you'll likely have less food.

Start with Realistic Expectations

When people find out I served my mission in the Fiji Islands, they usually ask, "How beautiful is the water," "Did I like the scuba diving," and "Which was my favorite resort?" I have to admit the tropical beaches were beautiful, but primarily because we used them for baptizing! You're not called to go on vacation, to take a break from life, or to explore the world—you are called to *serve*, and He expects you to work from sunup till sundown for the full duration of your mission. You're in this for the long haul, and that means long-term solutions and slow-moving progress. Your work is an investment whose dividends will mostly payoff in the long-term; you're running a marathon, not a 100-meter dash.

Keep It Positive

Elder Jeffrey R. Holland shared a personal maxim: "No misfortune is so bad that whining about it won't make it worse."[19] Don't complain or criticize, even in private to your companion. Negative words both flow from and create more negative thinking. Speak positively and hopefully and honor the Savior's admonition to "be of good cheer" (Matthew 14:27). As Orson F. Whitney once taught, "The spirit of the gospel is optimistic; it trusts in God and looks on the bright side of things. The opposite or pessimistic spirit drags men down and away from God, looks on the dark side, murmurs, complains, and is slow to yield obedience."[20] Be the kind of positive, cheerful person you would want to be around, and watch the happiness spread like sunshine.

At the same time, realize that it is completely normal to feel discouraged, homesick, lonely, depressed, and frustrated. Don't feel guilty when these feelings come. You need to learn how to recognize them, absorb them, let them move through you and away, and not dwell on them. Meditating on sad things is like using your faith backward; if you meditate on happy, outward things, you'll find success.

Keep Being Involved

Invest time in learning the local customs, traditions, and pastimes. When we had tribal cricket matches, harvesting/planting seasons, wedding ceremonies, or funeral services, we asked to attend where appropriate and participated as much as possible. Use your service hours to get involved in the peoples' lives, and let them know you are available to jump at any chance to work. Wherever you are, be *present*. When you're with members or at church meetings, keep your face out of your iPad, planner, or other books. Stay connected and in tune with what is happening around you. Members will respond positively when you are engaged, and less so when you are detached and aloof.

Keep a Record

Write in your journal every day, even if it's just a little bit. Try different writing prompts like "Today's highlight/lowlight . . ." "I never knew that . . ." "I've seen God's hand in . . ." "Today I learned . . ." "Tomorrow will be different because . . ." "This is the last time I . . ."

Build your own "topical guide" of scriptures to use when certain topics arise. I taped a blank sheet of paper inside the cover of my scriptures, and as certain topics would keep coming up in discussions, I'd note the topic and then make it a point of scripture study to find simple verses that addressed that topic and write them down. Having my own bulleted quick reference sheet helped a lot in future lessons, and eventually I had the scriptures all memorized.

Keep It Tidy

"The cleaner the home, the clearer the mind" is a good truism to follow. Three to five minutes of tidying every day can be more effective than hours of scrubbing once every other week. Many companionship frustrations can be avoided by simply committing to keep your home clean. And no matter how bad your day was, coming home to a messy house just makes it worse, while a clean place of rest can be a place of peace. Another good test is to ask yourself: "If our chapel was as clean as our apartment, would our investigators still want to get baptized?" So clean up your crap.

Make Lessons Memorable

The people you teach won't remember most names, dates, facts, or history points of gospel stuff. But they *will* remember general stories and how they felt when they heard them. Don't give history lessons, but rather try to find the humanity in the history. Show how people struggled and overcame with God's help, and connect the dots to how your investigators can overcome as well. Learn how to resolve concerns with the Book of Mormon— use it as often as you can. Spend study time developing your own personal, heartfelt responses to questions such as "Why do bad things happen to good people," "What happens after we die," "Why didn't God answer my prayers," "Why doesn't God send me a sign," and so on.

Make Time Count

Because that's what "MTC" *really* stands for. We had a saying in our mission: "if you're doing it right, the days will feel like years and the years will feel like days." You'll likely come home exhausted at night, wondering when will it ever end—only to look in the mirror one day and realize you're going home just when you're beginning to feel like you're making progress. So make sure you don't waste time doing unimportant or ineffective tasks. Plan your day's work, then work your plan. Use your downtime to review new vocabulary words, memorize scriptures, and read inspirational books (like this one! :-D). Keep your visits to members' homes tight, focused, and brief. Use P-day time to "unstring the bow" and give your mind and body time to recharge and refocus—then get ready to go out the next day and *carpé* the heck out of the *diem*.

Be Efficient and Effective

Most Church units have lists of inactive and part-member families, and many of them have likely not been visited by local leaders. These families can be "gold mines" of opportunities for sharing the gospel. Working with local members to find friends, close relatives, and extended family members can often yield so much potential work that there is little need for door-to-door contacting. Counsel with your ward mission leader to find out which ways of working have proven to be most efficient and effective.

Be Teachable

Everyone you meet knows something you don't. If you approach every relationship as a chance to learn, you'll grow in surprising but necessary ways. Seek input and feedback from others, and be willing to adopt their perspective. Keep learning, especially the doctrinal and historical points of your own faith. Admit your own faults

This is preparation for life later on; there are no transfers in marriage.

and acknowledge when you are wrong. Be ready to receive correction when you need to, and trust that those who would correct you are on your team. Listen to your coaches, even if they're yelling at you; they just want to help you win the game. Keeping a small notebook with you will allow you to take notes when you learn something new. (*If you really want to remember something, write it down.*)

Be Patient and Loving

When I was struggling with getting along with a particular companion, I wrote to the president, explaining our issues and suggesting/asking/pleading that we be split up and transferred. "I could work so much more effectively if I was with someone who wasn't holding me back!" I vainly asked. My president simply responded, "You will stay with him until you work out your issues. This is preparation for life later on; there are no transfers in marriage."

So we stuck it out, worked it out, and just when I had learned my lesson and had figured out how I needed to change in order to have a peaceful, happy relationship, we were transferred and split up. (Apparently I didn't learn my lesson—he became my companion again three months later!)

Do everything you can to develop charity and patience for your companion. Small things like polishing *their* shoes in addition to your own, complimenting him or her both in public and in private, and being interested in their lives and hobbies can go a long way in smoothing over relationships.

One missionary learned of all his junior companion's failing and obedience problems from the members in his branch. They tried complaining to the senior elder, listing all the things the junior was doing wrong and all the ways that he wasn't a good missionary, hoping that the senior would commiserate with them and give them a plan on how they could "fix" the junior companion. But instead he simply replied, "Yes, I know about his faults. And I love him anyway."

"Poisoning the well" is a phenomenon where Missionary #1 will tell Missionary #2 negative things about Missionary #3, so that Missionary #2 will be "well prepared" should he ever be companions with Missionary #3. The emotional and psychological damage from this proves to be a significant stumbling block in developing love, trust, charity, and friendship. Some companionships never recover, and the work suffers—so don't do it. If you hear someone trying to spread the dirt, kindly stop them, forget what they say, and give Missionary #3 a fair shake.

Boldness: Fake It Till You Make It

Love people enough to overcome your fear. Or as the scriptures say, "open your mouths and they shall be filled" (D&C 33:8). And in case you're *not* bold, try pretending you are for a day and just see what happens. Imagine what a bold person would do in a given situation—then try to act like them. Learn how to ask genuine ice-breaking questions about family, work, hobbies, and school as a way of starting conversations with people you don't know well. Learn which topics to avoid and which are most effective. Chances are the more experienced missionaries in your area could help you make a list of key topics that work well.

Bring a Grateful Heart

Great power is unlocked by a grateful heart. Start a habit of seeking out the good in every facet of your mission, even in the difficult areas, the hard work, the awkward companion, or the lack of investigators. Try not to be jealous of others that receive care packages or letters more often than you; there will *always* be someone worse off than you. Be gracious to anyone who invites you into their home. Whenever you've been invited to someone's home, remember the Three Commandments of Dinnertime:

1) Thou shalt not be late
2) Thou shalt always proclaim the meal to be delicious
3) Thou shalt be the first to offer to clean the dishes

One elder taught us that instead of sitting down and saying, "Can we do anything to help?" he would grab some things from the table and say, "Where can I put these?" Then he would roll up his sleeves and dig into the sink full of dishes. He had a particular knack for being charming, complimentary, gracious, and amiable. (He easily became a favorite of the Relief Society.) It's a skill anyone can learn, and doing so will pay great dividends.

Bring Your Own Flair

Be yourself and use whatever skills and talents you have to offer. It could be playing basketball, playing musical instruments, making yogurt, telling jokes, doing magic tricks, being a good listener, giving good advice, or just being a diligent, hard worker.

In one area we served, the locals were quite fascinated with Americans (they'd never met anyone who would come from so far away, just to live in their little corner of the island) and were curious about our customs and cuisine. So we learned how to make simple cakes and sweet breads from scratch and offered to drop by at tea-time and cook for them. Knowing how to make a handful of simple recipes from home is always a good idea. If your region is known for a specialty dish or unique cuisine, see if you can find someone to teach you how to make it. Also be able to sing a handful of your favorite hymns from memory.

Let Go of the Little Stuff

Most disagreements and interpersonal frictions are over very trivial items. I was very lucky when I met my first companion—our personalities just *clicked* and he was immeasurably patient and kind, so our weekly 'companionship inventory' (where we'd sit and bravely face whatever interpersonal conflicts we were struggling with) went like this:

"Hey man, I'm cool with you. You cool with me?"

"Yup. We're cool."

"Alright, cool. Love ya, bro."

Other elders in our area, however, would sit up for almost an hour, trying to keep their emotions under control as they laid out a tableau of nitpicking complaints about each other. Every time it happened I'd look at my companion with a *"Man, I'm glad you're patient with me"* glance. I realized that I, too, was doing some of the same things those other elders were complaining about, but my companion just chose to not be bothered with it. He later revealed his secret: "Just let go of the little stuff. *And remember: it's* all *little stuff.*"

Another elder gave me this tip: "When talking things out and trying to solve a personal problem with your companion, try to sit side by side, as if you're both looking at the problem together. That way if you shoot for the problem and miss, you don't accidentally hit your companion."

Let transfer time be a season of repentance as you reflect on what you could have done better and what you'll commit to do with your next companion. Let go of your old behaviors and start fresh with the best version of yourself you can summon.

Don't Hate Your Enemies

This includes loving those who disrespect or ridicule you, even if it's within the Church or mission. Sometimes the hardest ones to love and pray for will be those who mock or disrespect you for being obedient and hardworking. Don't give in to the "natural man" tendency

FAITH AND A LIFE JACKET

to snap back or fan the flames. Be ready to forgive them before they even offend you. Learn to disagree without being disagreeable, even if you genuinely feel you are right and they are wrong. As the old saying goes, holding on to a grudge is like drinking poison and expecting the other person to die.

Don't Be Stupid

Some of our elders in the MTC thought it would be fun to be sneaky, and one night they left their rooms and with some of their companions, broke in to a restricted area, and took pictures of themselves defacing the walls. They dropped off their film to be developed at the MTC bookstore, and when the staff there saw what the elders had done, they reported it to the mission president. All the elders were summoned, censured, and nearly sent home—all over a stupid indiscretion. What a waste it would have been had they lost their opportunity to serve!

Sometimes you'll see missionaries goofing around like ordinary teenagers would do. The only problem with that is you're not *supposed* to be ordinary—you're supposed to be different, even on P-day. You face more scrutiny and higher expectations than other young people your age. Your public behavior and the impression you leave behind will be inseparably connected to people's perceptions of the Church, so make sure it is dignified, positive, and uplifting. If you're ever unsure about whether you should proceed with a choice, err on the side of caution and control. Don't do anything you wouldn't want your mission president to know about. Relationships built slowly over a long time can come crumbling down in an instant by small lapses of judgment. **All it takes is one *"Oh, shoot . . ."* to undo a year's worth of *"atta boy"*s!**

Love Is All You Need

Please don't feel intimidated or overwhelmed by the list of suggestions above. Nobody is ever going to do *all* of that; just pick an area that you feel you could work on and make that a focus for your week. In the midst of all your growing social skills and learning how to be a functioning adult, remember that your undergirding motivation should be love for the people. That is the magic glue that binds all these skills together and directs them to be used for good. That sort of Christlike love suffers long, is kind, doesn't envy, isn't puffed up in pride, isn't easily provoked, doesn't think harshly of others, and doesn't rejoice in unhappiness or iniquity. That kind of love rejoices in truth, bears all trials, believes all that is true, hopes in all that is hopeful, and endures all challenges. It never fails. So if you can hold on to just one thing, hold on to charity, which is the greatest of all. It really is all you need (see Moroni 7:45–46).

GOING, SAYING, BEING

Joseph Smith once taught, "A man filled with the love of God, is not content with blessing his family alone, but ranges through the whole world, anxious to bless the whole human race."[21] We saw this love personified as we spent more and more time with the islanders. They were poor, but they were oh so happy. They had learned that happiness can come from helping each other not only survive but *thrive*. And when that desire to thrive was paired with the principles of the gospel of Christ, each family's outreach and impact on the community was amplified, multiplied, and expanded. Our members were known as good, kind-hearted leaders in the community. They were trustworthy employees, dedicated teachers, and open-minded neighbors who accepted those around them and loved them as God did. They had experienced the transformative power of Christ's grace in their own lives, and they radiated that same light out to others around them. Something was *different* about them.

As missionaries, there's a song that we'd sing whose meaning gradually changed for me over time. (*Funny how that works out, isn't it? Go back and read your favorite scripture or your patriarchal blessing every four to six months or so and see if its meaning hasn't shifted for you too.*) It's hymn number 270, "I'll Go Where You Want Me to Go." There's a subtle progression throughout the verses that we saw reflected in the lives of the members and missionaries who dedicated their whole heart to the work—it's a progression of **going**, **saying**, and **being**.

We'd start our missions by answering the Lord's call, with our hands in His, that we'll go where He wants us to **go**. But every once in a while we'd have a missionary who was there in body but not in heart or mind. They seemed reluctant to dive in and let themselves be transformed by the work. Sometimes they'd be preoccupied with life back home or would be hesitant to engage in the rules and the work. It was as if something was holding them back.

As we kept working and serving, we eventually learned that there are "loving words that Jesus would have us speak" to those wandering in paths of sin. We learned that we could follow the rules and the programs, learn the discussions, and learn the common questions and answers. If we relied on Him to be our guide, our voices would echo the sweet message of Christ's gospel as we said what He wanted us to **say**.

But even that wasn't always enough. We saw missionaries who would talk their way through a lesson, but sometimes their testimonies would lack power or personal conviction. It was easy for some elders to say the right things and follow the scripts of missionary life, but when their personal actions didn't line up with what they were teaching, their sayings rang hollow.

Finally it *clicked* for me, the meaning of that song.

Anyone can just *go* through motions of being a missionary.

But not everyone has the mission experience really go *through them*.

Anyone can memorize a handful of scriptures or craft a well-tuned sermon or talk, or just *say* what they're supposed to. But not everyone allows those words of life to be engraved on their heart as deeply as they are in their minds.

The entire point of being a missionary isn't just about going or saying—it's about *being*. It's about truly trusting our *all*—not 90 percent, not even 99 percent, but our *all*—to His tender care and having perfect confidence that He loves us. And because He loves us, and we have trusted Him enough to put our entire heart, might, mind, and strength on the altar of missionary sacrifice, the enabling power of His Atonement will grad-

> **Not everyone allows those words of life to be engraved on their heart as deeply as they are in their minds.**

ually transform us into truer disciples of Christ. The change will be slow, almost imperceptible, but the metamorphosis is real. When this happens, you will find yourself reacting more kindly in stressful situations and more ready to not only offer kind words to solve the problems you face, but to break a sweat and earn a blister in seeing the problem solved yourself. You will become more accepting of those who are outcast, more tolerant of those who are divisive, and more ready to serve those who are in need. You'll find yourself wanting to help people in the ways they need most, even if they're not the most obvious. You will realize that you need to repent as much as those you teach, and that life is a constant struggle of perpetual improvement and refinement. You will be quick to offer sincere gratitude for even the smallest kindness, and you'll find that cheerfulness and friendliness come more naturally. You'll forgive those who offend you before they even ask for forgiveness, and you'll become less sensitive to offending situations. You'll know what it means to mourn with those who mourn, to comfort those who need comfort, and to bear another's burden. You will experience a refinement that reaches to every edge of your character.

The change won't happen auto-magically or without consistent effort and sacrifice. But by loving as Christ loved and serving as He served, by doing His will with a heart sincere, you'll become what He wants you to be.

Love the people. There is no substitute.

Sectarian priests often asked concerning Joseph, "How can this babbler get so many followers around him and retain them?" The Prophet answered, "It's because I possess the principle of love. All I have to offer the world is a good heart and a good hand."[22]

TRUTH #6

Success Ain't What You Think; God Measures It Differently

"The easier something is to measure, the less it's truly worth."

ALL THAT GLITTERS IS NOT GOLD

Before I was allowed to fly out to the islands, I had to wait for my international visa to be prepared and approved. The process got bogged down in paperwork and took longer than necessary, so when my time at the MTC had finished and my visa still wasn't ready, I was sent to a stateside mission to work for a time while I waited. There I came face-to-face with an uncomfortable facet of our culture—the tendency to equate numbers and measurable progress with faith and obedience. In this particular area, success was determined by statistics.

Each companionship was given a series of numerical targets to achieve during their daily work: the number of pass-along cards distributed, new people met, discussions given, copies of the Book of Mormon passed out, and so on. Every night the missionaries were required to phone their leaders with their numbers for the day, which were then rolled up to a master report at the mission office. The missionaries who hit their daily targets were praised as being "successful," while those who didn't were given additional "coaching" in an effort to increase their numbers. The mission also recommended each missionary set personal numerical targets, such as the number of scripture verses memorized, how many investigators were brought to church, or the number of converts baptized.

That last statistic—baptisms—was the big target that everyone naturally shot for. The mission encouraged progress toward a specific number of baptisms by giving a golden name tag to anyone who achieved it. This highly coveted "pot of gold" became the insignia separating the successful missionaries from the unsuccessful. At zone conferences a natural form of segregation began to occur between those with gold badges and those without—like Dr. Seuss's star-bellied Sneeches, who had "stars upon thars." Missionaries excitedly talked about who was close to getting "gilded" and debated whether "non-gold" missionaries should ever be in leadership positions. Some of them would share strategies for increasing their numbers and hoped to be sent to the easy areas where baptisms seemed to be plentiful.

One day I was on splits with a very energetic, hard-working zone leader who was determined to show me what a "good missionary" was. We nearly jogged from door to door as we canvased a neighborhood handing out pamphlets and books, speeding down roads as we visited investigators and less-actives, only stopping to catch our breath for a minute as we wolfed down a fast food burger for both lunch and dinner. He quizzed me on scripture memorization while we drove, tested me on the discussions, and tried to coach me on the best techniques for turning wishy-washy investigators into committed converts. His energetic dedication to the work and frantic zeal to not waste a moment of time was certainly praiseworthy, but something about his hectic pace and burning focus on numbers really bugged me.

We were chatting about goals and life plans at the end of our workday, waiting for my regular companion to meet up with us again, and I asked him what he really *wanted* from his mission, and he responded with a surprising answer.

He looked out the car window, lost in thought for a moment, and said wistfully, "My goal is to baptize fifty people by the end of my mission."

Just then my companion arrived and I had to leave, so I never got to continue the conversation with the zone leader. As he drove off, I finally put my finger on it. I couldn't help but wonder, *Wait, what happens if you only baptize twenty people? Or forty? Or even forty-nine? Does that mean you'd feel like a failure? Would it all have been a waste? What if you only baptized one single person? Or what if you spent your whole mission doing everything you were supposed to, and nobody joined, through no fault of your own? What then? Would you feel like you were still successful?*

I began to understand the difference between missionaries who are focused on *statistics* versus those who are focused on *souls*. One missionary, when asked how many people she had seen baptized, proudly puffed up her chest and proclaimed "Twenty!" Another missionary, when asked the same question, replied, "Let me think . . . there was Pierre and his wife, and Andrea. We also taught the Jones family, and I've heard that the Bobby Smith from my last area is coming back to Church, so that's great."

Do you see the difference?

It's easy to let the numbers of your mission be the yardstick by which you measure your progress, but don't let those fool you into focusing on the wrong things. Just because a car's gas gauge reads "full" doesn't mean that the tires have enough air or the engine has enough oil or that you are driving at the proper speed; one metric alone isn't sufficient data to establish the overall health of an entire system.

In Doctrine and Covenants 18:16, the Lord invited Joseph Smith and the early Saints to envision just how great will be their joy if they bring "many souls" unto Him. While foreseeing future success and visualizing how we achieve it is certainly a key skill to develop, we shouldn't overlook the message of the preceding verse. "If it so be that you should labor all your days in crying repentance unto this people, and bring, save it be one soul unto me, how great shall be your joy with him in the kingdom of my Father!" (D&C 18:15). Like the parables of the shepherd who leaves the ninety-nine to seek out the one, or the widow woman who sweeps her whole house to find a single lost drachma, Christ is eternally focused on the *one*. He didn't perform the miraculous Atonement just for the billions of God's children collectively—He completed it on an individual, case-by-case basis, one soul at a time. His joy in a single heart returning to Him is no less than if an entire nation bowed in repentance. Salvation in Christ is an intimate, individual, and beautifully personal experience that can't be rushed, measured, or established by quotas.

Truth #6: Success ain't what you think.

COMPARISON IS THE THIEF OF JOY

Even though the zone conferences in the islands of New Caledonia didn't have golden name tags or special rewards for the number of baptisms, they were still an opportunity to share the progress we were making in each area. As my senior companion shared the success we were having with the chiefs in Lifou, the *elders* all clapped and cheered for us. But I noticed that they would also cheer just as loudly for *anyone's* accomplishments, no matter how great or small. The mission there had established a culture of being genuinely happy for other's success. Their joy wasn't found in boasting of their own accomplishments and taking pride in what *they* had done, but in listening to the struggles and successes of *others* and in giving congratulatory praise to everyone else. The more they focused their energy outward and less on themselves, the happier they were. It took me a long time to realize that I had been following the default script of the Scarcity Mentality, while they were following the script of the Abundance Mentality.

Stephen Covey explained it this way:

> Most people are deeply scripted in what I call the Scarcity Mentality. They see life as having only so much, as though there were only one pie out there. And if someone were to get a big piece of the pie, it would mean less for everybody else. . . . People with a Scarcity Mentality have a very hard time being genuinely happy for the success of other people—even, and sometimes especially, members of their own family.
>
> The Abundance Mentality, however, flows out of a deep inner sense of personal worth and security. It is the paradigm that there is plenty out there and enough to spare for everybody. It results in sharing of prestige, of recognition, of profits, of decision making. It opens possibilities, options, alternatives, and creativity.[23]

So here's the secret to making missionary work more enjoyable:

don't treat it like a zero-sum game, where one person can win only if everyone else loses. Instead, treat it like highly-interactive co-op adventure, where all the missionaries and members are on the same team, up against the whole wide world. The game started long before you jumped in, and it will keep going when you jump out and someone else takes your spot. A victory for anyone one person on your mission is a victory for *everyone*, so celebrate each other's victories, no matter how small. Don't give in to the temptation of thinking that others' lights have to dim in order for yours to shine out the brighter. Instead, coax their light, cup it in your hands, protect it from the winds, and help it grow—and you'll see your own blaze brilliantly as well. Disciples of Christ enjoy an inter-connected-ness of soul and purpose when they learn to knit their hearts together as one.

The prophet Alma understood this concept when he taught his followers after their escape from King Noah. He knew that their very survival required meaningful interdependence; he insisted that his newly ordained priests both lived it and taught it to others.

> And he commanded them that there should be no contention one with another, but that they should look forward with one eye, having one faith and one baptism, having their hearts knit together in unity and in love one towards another.
>
> And thus he commanded them to preach. And thus they became the children of God. (Mosiah 18:21–22)

I love the imagery of their hearts being "knit together in unity and love." It's a very fitting metaphor: if you pick at one piece of a knitted sweater and start pulling apart the thread, eventually the entire creation will fall to pieces. Only by carefully, skillfully knit-ting together the weak individual threads can a new, sturdy, and warm garment be created. Every thread is vital and not a single stitch is inconsequential. The gospel of Christ thrives in just such a cul-ture, where struggles are shared, challenges are co-championed, and honors are humbly deflected and diffused.

When caught in the paradigm of the Scarcity Mentality, it's quite common to compare yourself to others through a very dis-torted lens. In doing so you'll likely magnify your own faults and flaws and minimize your strengths and accomplishments, while doing the exact opposite to everyone else's. Such a distorted perspective will reflect your true success about as accurately as a carnival fun house mirror reflects your true appearance, bending and disfiguring your identity into a warped version of the truth. What's scary about such contraptions is that if you look at them long enough, you may eventually believe they are true!

No matter how long we have gazed into such twisted mirrors and believed such a mangled representation of ourselves, we can always turn to God and rely on His power to strip away the false reflections and reset our true self-image. He alone has the power to "look on the heart" and see us as we truly are. By returning to His light often we may gain His perspective and see the beauty that is abundant in all of us and the plentiful blessings that are available to everyone.

During your mission you will be constantly reminded about the primal need for obedience and how obeying God's commandments can open the windows of Heaven and unlock miracles. But there's a good possibility that you'll meet missionaries who are disobedient and are still able to baptize.

You will likely have periods of intense fasting and constant prayer while begging for a miracle to happen in the lives of your investigator, only to see other missionaries who don't seem to work as hard still get the miracle.

Sometime you may feel frustrated that despite all your obedience and hard work, the heavens don't open for you how or when you want. Sometimes it just won't seem fair.

In the midst of these seeming imbalances, please remember that God's laws don't follow the same sort of cause-and-effect rules that our mortal lives are bound by. Faith and obedience aren't tokens to a sort of celestial vending machine that merely dispenses blessings once we've paid a high enough price. We don't get to choose how God will respond to our obedience, including whether or not He'll reward us with a blessing. And *no one's* faith, no matter how strong, will ever cause God to override someone else's free agency. If other missionaries are having more success than you, it is not an indicator that you are unworthy, disobedient, faithless, or are not good enough as a missionary. The outward, visible results of missionary work never truly reveal all the inward, invisible efforts and struggles that may take years to overcome. If you are overly focused on waiting to receive one particular type of blessing, you may become blind to the many other ways the Lord blesses your life without being asked. Don't let tunnel vision prevent you from seeing God's hand around you.

It has been said "Comparison is the thief of joy," and rarely will you see this for yourself as much as when you gather with other missionaries. Please resist the desire to compare and contrast your efforts and results, lest you be robbed of the joy that comes from humble service. Keep your self-esteem grounded in who you are and why you are there, knowing that God rewards all who offer their talents in his employ, whether they be great or small in number.

THE SONS OF LEHI

I have an older brother who was a rock-solid example to me of a what a good, hardworking, obedient missionary should be. His stories and letters made a deep impression on my mind, because I was only two years behind him in the family line and would be leaving for my own mission before he came home from his. While he was in the MTC, he shared an insight with me that shaped my own missionary service.

Don't let tunnel vision prevent you from seeing God's hand around you.

He told me that he noticed a natural sorting among the missionaries at the MTC and in his mission field. Not that he was trying to judge every missionary he met or categorize them into one bucket or another, but that there were very distinct patterns of behavior that naturally repeated over and over again. I saw the same patterns as well on my mission years later, and chances are you will see them on your mission too, no matter where you serve. It's the pattern of the sons of Lehi—Laman, Lemuel, Sam, and Nephi. It looks like this:

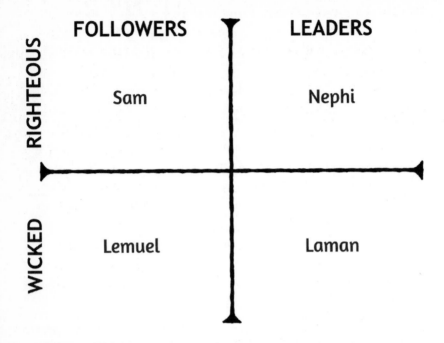

The four quadrants represent the major archetypes of behaviors we saw among the missionaries and members alike. Thankfully, the most common types of missionaries we saw were the Nephis and Sams—the men and women who stood up, stood out, spoke up, and worked out their salvation by bringing the gospel to those around them. They were obedient, humble, dedicated, and diligent in their efforts to be true Leaders and Followers of Righteousness. Now, to be honest, they weren't perfect in all things, they didn't all have 100 percent stable testimonies, and they made their share of mistakes along the way. But they were genuinely willing to do their best, and their continued efforts at personal refinement and improvement showed their consecration to discipleship.

Unfortunately, we also had missionaries that were more like Laman and Lemuel, the Leaders and Followers of Wickedness. Sometimes they would fall into habits of disobedience, pride, apathy, or neglect. Many of them had poor habits from pre-mission life that they brought with them in to the field. Some of them had poor role models as missionary trainers or weren't properly instructed. Others just made downright dumb decisions and had no regard for the mission rules, programs, and procedures. Rebellion came natural and easy to them; one even told me that he just didn't feel like he "fit in" when trying to be an obedient, hard-working missionary. "That's just not me," he said sadly.

When I first heard about these sorts of struggles, I thought their choices of intentional disobedience were perhaps an exaggeration. *Surely you wouldn't go on a mission only to wind up intentionally breaking rules and wasting time?* I thought. But the reality is that people are very complicated creatures, their personal backgrounds are often messy, their issues are complex and three-dimensional, and most of the time they're still trying to figure out life and how to improvise their way through adulthood, just like the rest of us.

While it may seem strange to have such diverse degrees of obedience in the mission field, I gradually understood it was part of God's plan all along. He didn't intend for us to roll off a missionary-prep assembly line and drop uniformly into prepackaged proselyting trappings like a fresh batch of white-shirted clones. Nope—when He called us to serve Him, He allowed us to bring with us all the weaknesses and struggles and personality quirks, and yes, even sins and troubles we were still carrying. He doesn't wait until we are perfect; He calls us because we are *perfectible*. He is fully aware of our imperfections, but He knows that even though we may be "small and simple," and the "weak things of the earth," full of flaws and foibles, we can still bring to pass many things which are great—*if* we are willing to correct ourselves and move to the Righteous quadrants (Alma 37:6, D&C 124:1). God is the best at making lemonade out of lemons, because that's all He has.

The Book of Mormon teaches this doctrine beautifully: "I give unto men weakness that they may be humble; and my grace is sufficient for all men that humble themselves before me; for if they humble themselves before me, and have faith in me, then will I make weak things become strong unto them" (Ether 12:27). Whatever unnecessary spiritual baggage we may bring with us to the mission field, God invites us to leave it at His feet and move onward and upward. By striving to move along the spectrum of righteousness and leadership, committing ourselves every day to improve one small weakness at a time, we'll find ourselves gradually refined, polished, and perfected.

Now, bear in mind that simply going through the motions of missionary work won't cut it. Laman and Lemuel did many of the right things for the wrong reasons and thus missed out on the transformational blessings that could have been theirs. It's possible to climb the holy mountain of God without becoming truly elevated within. Just like Nephi and Sam, Laman and Lemuel gave up their riches, left their homelands behind, built a ship, and crossed the waters. On occasion they even repented of their mistakes and humbly called on the Lord for assistance. But the tragedy of their story is that they were so focused on selfish rebellion, rather than faithful obedience and charity, that they were unable to mature in the gospel and grow up unto Christ, instead being left to "become for themselves" (3 Nephi 1:29).

Consider the words of Elder David A. Bednar, speaking of this process of becoming something better:

> The issue is not going to church; rather, the issue is worshipping and renewing covenants as we attend church. The issue is not going to or through the temple; rather, the issue is having in our hearts the spirit, the covenants, and the ordinances of the Lord's house. The issue is not going on a mission; rather, the issue is *becoming a missionary* and serving throughout our entire life with all of our heart, might, mind, and strength.[24]

Laman and Lemuel's blindness came from a simple source: "they knew not the dealings of that God who had created them" (1 Nephi 2:12). Because they didn't truly understand the nature of *God*, they never truly understood *themselves*,[25] their weaknesses and strengths, or how a partnership with their Creator could alchemize more of the former into the latter. Their hearts and minds were so fixed on the past and promises of inheritance and property, on things they could hold and count, on dreams of comfort, wealth, and happiness, that they were never able to see the vision that their parents and brothers saw—a future of blessings immeasurable, of sustenance despite discomfort, of riches celestial, and of joy eternal. While Laman's eyes looked backward to the forfeited lands of his inheritance, Nephi looked forward to the land of promise and beyond, to the joy of entering in to the presence of the Lord. Nephi knew that the measure of his discipleship would be found in the intangible, the unmeasurable.

So as you find yourself at different points along that righteousness quadrant, be reminded of just Whom you have committed to serve. Take a long look at your name tag: your name and His, side by side. He knows your heart, knows what it can become, and if you let Him, He will help you become not just a Follower of Righteousness but a Leader.

GOD MEASURES IT DIFFERENTLY

So, back to the story of the mission area with the gold badges. It turns out that they also had a lot of leaders focused on the *inward* signs of conversion—I was just too fixated on judging the guys who were trying to pad their statistics to realize that many of the people there were actually focused on the right things. (Like most flaws and weaknesses, it was very easy to recognize the problem in others rather than seeing it in myself and having the courage to own it and clean it up. I'm still trying to work on that. :-/)

I had my first real taste of learning how to recognize this inward conversion when we wanted to baptize the children of a family who had been inactive for a time. Actually, it was their parents who wanted us to teach their kids, so we jumped at the chance, thinking we'd get an easy baptism and maybe reactivate the parents too. We set an early baptism date for them and looked forward to counting their numbers toward our monthly goal.

But a very wise bishop got in our way.

He insisted on having the *entire* family come back to church, for multiple consecutive visits, all on their own, before he would consider interviewing the kids for baptism and allowing them to join. He wanted to see how well they would continue in the path of discipleship once the missionaries were no longer involved. He didn't just want them in the water, so to speak—he wanted them planted deep in the ground of the gospel. Of course, this was totally going to throw off our numbers for the month. Not cool.

"Doesn't he understand that we *need* them to get baptized next week?" our zealous zone leader said over the phone with us. He was listening to our explanation of why the family's baptism date had fallen through and been pushed back several weeks. He decided to come to ward council with us and plead his case with the bishop, assuring us that he'd be able to change the leaders' minds. Once the ward leaders knew of our zone's baptism goal, surely they'd give in and let the baptism happen right?

Heh . . . not even.

The bishop held his ground. He knew that if we tried harvesting the fruit before it was ready, it would likely spoil. He was concerned with commitment and conversion, not just statistics and goals. He believed that progress in the gospel was measured by how a person changed their life to align with God's will in *all* areas, not just in taking the single step of baptism. He truly wanted to share in our success but he wanted that success to *last*, because once we were gone, that family would still be his responsibility and their struggle would continue. He knew that if any victory were to be had, it would need to be the long-term triumph shared by convert and member alike as they knit their hearts together in unity.

So, grudgingly at first, we followed his counsel and worked with the family for many, many weeks. It took a long time before they were unified and committed enough to have their children join.

But once they did, they were *solid*.

That was the kind of success we were looking for. And even though our monthly numbers were low and we never hit our baptism goal, we felt like we'd still nailed the bull's-eye because we had worked with them through their conversion in the *best* way, not just the *fastest*.

President Gordon B. Hinckley shared this counsel: "Do your very, very best. Say your prayers and work hard, and leave the harvest to the Lord."[26] You will find that as you honestly put forth your best effort, you will grow in confidence that you are a successful missionary regardless of whether or not people accept your message and no matter how meager your monthly numbers may be. After all, the great missionary anthem doesn't say "Called to

A heart full of gratitude will not have room for jealousy of others or pity for itself.

baptize everyone in this town!" No, it simply says "Called to serve Him." And we serve Him by humbly, diligently serving those around us, helping them along at whatever their own spiritual pace is.

A heart full of gratitude will not have room for jealousy of others or pity for itself, but will cheer with those who bring home the prodigal and rejoice when the lost become found, regardless of who helps find them or how long it has been since their return. There is truth in the words of *Preach My Gospel*, which states, "When you have done your very best, you may still experience disappointments, but you will not be disappointed in yourself. You can feel certain that the Lord is pleased when you feel the Spirit working through you. Your success as a missionary is primarily measured by your commitment."[27]

Success ain't what you think; God measures it differently.

When the Lord measures an individual, He does not take a tape measure around the person's head to determine his mental capacity, nor his chest to determine his manliness, but He measures the heart as an indicator of the person's capacity and potential to bless others.

—Marvin J. Ashton[28]

TRUTH #7

Forget Yourself and Go to Work

"Yes, men and women who turn their lives over to God will discover that He can make a lot more out of their lives than
they can. He will deepen their joys, expand their vision,
quicken their minds, strengthen their muscles, lift their spirits,
multiply their blessings, increase their opportunities, comfort
their souls, raise up friends, and pour out peace.
"Whoever will lose his life in the service of God will find eternal life."
—Ezra T. Benson[29]

"There is no tragedy in all the ages like the everyday
tragedy of men who fall short of their possibilities."
—Gordon B. Hinckley[30]

DEAR JOHN'D

Before my mission I was dating a girl that I was convinced was
the one for me.

Emphasis on *was* dating. She dumped me while I was away.
Here's how it all went down.

We had met in marching band and had been dating for about
a year before I left. During that time we hadn't really talked about
plans for the future or done the whole DTR thing, because we both
just *knew* that we'd be together afterward.

Or at least, we thought we knew.

On the day of my mission farewell, she and a big group of high school friends all came over to my house for the traditional good-bye party. She was the last one to leave that afternoon. We hugged it out and she finally walked away, up the long hill that was our driveway. I stood at the bottom, empty as a shell, not sure of what was going to happen next but absolutely certain that my heart was breaking.

She turned around at the top of the hill, saw me standing there. I could see her put her hand to her face and just shake her head, and then she came running back down to me.

"I just can't do this," she panted as she hugged me tight.

I held her again, not knowing how to respond.

She quieted down, reached into her reservoir of courage, and looked up at me.

"Here's the truth," she said, taking a deep breath. "Neither of us knows what's going to happen in the future. So let's not pretend we can make plans."

Wait . . . is she breaking up with me? Where is this going? I thought.

She steadied her voice and continued. "It would be foolish of us to try to make promises today that may never come to pass. I mean, who knows what's going to happen?"

Dang it . . . she's making sense again. I sighed.

She laid out the rest of her idea. "So here's what we're going to do," she said. "You promise me that you will be 100 percent obedient to every single mission rule. You work your hardest. Do your absolute best. Don't complain, don't whine. Work hard and just leave everything you have out on the field."

"Okay, I can do that . . ." I answered.

"I will promise you that I will be 100 percent obedient to every commandment and counsel that I have here at home. I'll go to school, get a job, have a great life, stay active in the Church, keep growing spiritually, and do everything God wants me to do. At the end of your two years, let's see where we wind up. If I'm still single, let's get together and see what happens."

"But . . ." she paused and took my face in her hands, looking pleadingly into my eyes.

"If, during those two years, I get called away to be with my future companion, *you have to trust me that it's the right thing for both of us, and that that's what God wants."*

She seemed to be summoning every ounce of resolve to face down that fear, the fear that our hopes of a future together might evaporate. But she also knew that trying to avoid or ignore that possibility would only set us up for even greater pain.

I couldn't help but chuckle through my tears as I answered. "Well now, I guess that's just really the only logical thing we can do, now, isn't it? Stay obedient and see what happens."

So with a plan in place we said one last good-bye and hoped for the best.

A wise brother in my ward once told me, "The first part of your life is to get ready for your mission. Your mission, however, is to help you get ready for the rest of your life. So don't blow it."

Another one pointed out Spencer W. Kimball's famous "Lock Your Heart" talk and told me, "Either lock it up so girls don't come in, or if you already have one in there, lock it down so she doesn't come out and distract you."

I resolved that night to keep both of those counsels and give my mission my all. I wanted to hit the ground running, fully prepared, and leave everything on the table, holding nothing back. I wanted to come back thoroughly spent, used up, worn down, and wrung out of all I held dear, with the faith that in doing so I would be transformed, renewed, and evolved into something higher, something deeper.

So I left. And I left her. I actually put a small padlock on my backpack zipper as a reminder that my thoughts and dreams of her were "locked up." I gave her the key the day I flew out to the islands. She wore it on a necklace.

We stayed in touch for a time and wrote simple letters to each other. I tried my hardest to focus on the work.

Transfers. Airplanes. Catamarans. Island jungles, grass huts, angry natives, chases, escapes, true love, miracles. Through all this, for the first time in my life, I was threatened with death. And I had to ask myself whether I would endure it. For the first time I truly started to learn about Brother Joseph and to learn what it meant to study deeply from the well of eternal life. For the first time, I truly began to understand "doctrine." And I began to catch a tiny, candle-sized glimpse of the power of heaven and the magnitude of eternity.

Then her letters started to change and took longer to arrive.

"I got the job I really wanted, and I'm meeting new people . . . but I'm still yours." More waiting between letters.

"I'm so grateful for all the memories we made together."

"I'm learning so much about myself," she would say.

That last one scared me. *What do you mean you're "learning about yourself"? What are you learning? And who the heck is teaching you?!*

Then the letters stopped.

Maybe she stopped writing altogether, I thought. Or maybe they were just held up with the island postage. (Sometimes they would take over month to get delivered, and we had no internet access.)

Finally, one day a large envelope arrived. She had addressed it to "Elder Bernards," instead of using my first name like she usually did. *That's not a good sign,* I thought. She had sealed it on the back with her favorite sealing wax and signet imprint. She had only done that on rare occasions before.

I smiled nervously at my companion as he watched me open the letter. Something in my stomach started to flutter and get queasy.

"Dear Elder Bernards . . ." she began. She never began like that. *Oh no.*

"I will not mince words. Our paths are no longer the same."

I can't believe I'm reading this.

"So free your heart. Free your mind. Concentrate on the work. I'll always be grateful for the time we shared."

And that was it. She was gone.

I started getting dizzy. The room was spinning. I felt like the ground under me was rolling and I couldn't make sense of anything. I staggered to a couch and steadied myself as I sat down.

"Dude, what's *wrong* with you?" asked my companion, sitting there watching me. He was munching on a baguette and licking jam off his fingers.

"Um, I think I just got 'Dear John'd,'" I replied, in a whisper.

"Oh man . . . oh man, oh man, you've got to be *kidding* me! Oh that sucks. I'm so sorry."

I looked around frantically, trying to keep myself from spinning out of control. I felt like everything was coming unhinged. All the plans and hopes and dreams I had locked away were bursting out of that secure enclave in my heart, trying to tip me completely over.

I wrestled with the rest of the mail stack, looking for an escape, desperate to find anything else to read, something else to change the reality I was facing.

And there I found another letter for me, from my favorite cousin. I tore it open and scanned the surface, not really reading it but just letting my eyes race around the page while I wished the Dear John letter would just magically vanish.

She mailed that letter a month ago. She's already been gone for four weeks. It's over, and I can't do anything about it. It's totally over. Is this what I'm supposed to do, God? Just let it go and somehow be okay with it?

And then my eyes locked on a sentence from my cousin's letter:

"Hi Elder Bernards! Here's a cool quote I heard in my religion class today, from Joseph Smith. Hope it helps you!

'Whatever God asks is right, no matter what it is, even though we may not understand the reasons why until after the events have transpired.' "[31]

And the spinning world stopped.

Everything became eerily quiet and calm. It felt like the universe was holding its breath as I was weighed in a sort of cosmic scale, waiting to see how I would respond to this new challenge. I didn't truly realize how much I needed someone until I was asked to let them go and move on.

I tearfully looked up. *Father, is this really how it works? I have to choose? Do I sacrifice her and everything we had? Is it really going to be better for us if I do? I mean, I know I had sort of promised her that I would, but I guess I never realized it would come to this, or that it would hurt this much.*

And I remembered her words from what felt like a lifetime ago:

"If, during those two years, I get called away to be with my future companion, you have to trust me that it's the right thing for both of us, and that it's what God wants."

The way forward and upward became crystal clear to me. I

took a deep breath, walked back to the quiet darkness of my hut and closed the door. I slowly picked through my bags, gathering every letter and photo or anything else that reminded me of her. *This has to be a complete, 100 percent sacrifice*, I thought. *Nothing held back.*

With my hands full of memories, I made my way through the jungle to the cooking area in the clearing behind the hut. *Time to put it all on the altar and put the Lord to the test*, I thought.

We piled up the stones, the wood, and then the photos, images, letters, mementoes. Poured on oil. Lit the flame.

And walked away. Yeah, it was totally one of those slow-motion, action hero shots.

I found a sharpening file we used on our hunting machetes, and a few seconds later the "lock my heart" padlock came off my backpack.

I took a deep breath, feeling free and exposed and vulnerable. Terrified. Calm. Faithful and full of an optimistic hope that I'd never felt before.

"Dude, you okay?" asked my companion, who watched the whole (probably overdramatic) ritual with an awestruck kind of grin on his face.

"Yeah man, I'm fine. Let's get to work."

From that day forward, I finally felt *free* to focus 100 percent on the work. I learned how to rely on God and lose myself in His service like never before. My mission became a deeper, richer experience than anything I could have imagined earlier, all because I had to endure the pain of sacrificing one of the things that was the most precious to me.

I got Dear John'd. And it turned out to be the best thing that could have happened.

WHAT GORDON LEARNED THAT DAY

Now, that's not to say that getting over her was auto-magically easy or that the rest of my mission became instantly better. It still took time to move through the pain and feel like I was myself again. But the self that emerged was wholly different and the process of moving on seemed to happen faster than I anticipated. I think it's because of a very important lesson I learned from the mission experiences of Gordon B. Hinckley.

His family had scrimped and saved to put him through college during the middle of the Great Depression. His mom had died of cancer three years earlier, his dad was very busy as the stake president, his own savings had been wiped out when the local bank had failed, and every last family penny was treated as sacred and carefully accounted for. In the middle of this extreme financial hardship, his bishop approached him with what seemed like a shocking suggestion: Gordon should go on a mission. And he was called to England, which at the time was the most expensive mission in the world. He had no idea how he was supposed to leave his family, girlfriend, schooling, and job and then somehow raise enough money to pay for his mission. It seemed like an impossible challenge.

Then they discovered their sweet, late mother had secretly left a small savings account for Gordon's mission. She had been squirreling away change from grocery purchases and other shopping, should he someday decide to go. With that seed of savings and the family's combined sacrifices, Gordon was able to afford the mission.

The boat ride to England was long and uncomfortable. Gordon became seasick and homesick and was not well when he arrived. To make matters worse, he was sent to an area whose previous missionaries had been sent home because of violation of mission rules. The people in the city had known of their bad behavior, which only aggravated their antagonism toward Gordon and the other Mormons. He said of his first street meeting, "I was terrified. I stepped up on that little stand and looked at that crowd of people that had gathered. They were dreadfully poor at that time in the bottom of the Depression. They looked rather menacing and mean, but I somehow stumbled through whatever I had to say. We didn't get anywhere. To get people to listen to us was like knocking on a brick wall; they were bitter."

After only a week or two, Gordon had decided he'd had enough. Discouraged, he wrote home to his father and said he wanted to stop wasting everyone's time and what little money his father had and couldn't he just come home?

Two weeks later he received his father's terse reply. It was direct and to the point and contained the most important lesson a missionary could learn. His words are the core of **Truth #7:**

"Dear Gordon," his father replied, "I have your letter. I have only one suggestion:

Forget yourself and go to work."

LOSE YOURSELF

The same day he received his father's letter, Gordon came across this familiar statement during his personal scripture study: "For whosoever will save his life shall lose it; and whosoever will lose his life for my sake shall find it" (Matthew 16:25).

He decided to put the words of the Savior and his father to the test and offer himself up as a dedicatory sacrifice.

> With my father's letter in hand, I went into our bedroom in the house at 15 Wadham Road, where we lived, and got on my knees and made a pledge with the Lord. I covenanted that I would try to forget myself and lose myself in His service.
>
> That July day in 1933 was my day of decision. A new light came into my life and a new joy into my heart. The fog of England seemed to lift, and I saw the sunlight. I had a rich and wonderful mission experience, for which I shall ever be grateful.[32]

This paradox occurs frequently in scripture, and you may find it hard to believe to be true. Once tested and tried, however, you will find the transforming grace of God that is only accessible when we let go of old habits, prejudices, preferences, and self-imposed limitations and square up beneath the cross of Christ. You may already know that the purpose of a yoke is to get animals to pull together to move a large load.

Truth #7: Forget yourself and go to work.

Harnessing their strength with a yoke does indeed give them an extra burden, but the resulting productive force is greater than the sum of their individual strength; the yoke synergizes their efforts and multiplies their abilities. So if you were to "yoke" yourself with Christ in your missionary work, just imagine what miracles you could accomplish with Him at your side! His yoke is "easy" in the sense that it can become easier to overcome challenges and unlock your potential with Him, rather than doing it alone. Having His strength on your side means you won't have to transform under nothing but your own power, but transforming requires courage to let go of your past.

Part of the magical experience of being on a mission is that the environment is very conducive to new beginnings and fresh restarts. If you choose to truly dedicate yourself to the work, you will find it easy to set aside thoughts of school, work, family, loved ones, future plans, or troubles at home. God assures us that such things will be handled with care and that we can trust His oversight and awareness of our needs. In the Doctrine and Covenants, He assures Sidney Rigdon and Joseph that their "families are well; they are in my hands, and I will do them as seemeth me good" (D&C 100:1), and we can take comfort that His love likewise extends to each of us.

If you have ever felt the stirrings of peace and love in your heart when working on a service project, offering a loving hand to someone in need, or simply being aware of another's pain and sympathizing with them, then you know what it means to find new vitality by giving of your own life's energy to others. As children of the same Heavenly Parents, our souls have the ability to resonate harmoniously with others as we attune to *Them* and de-center from *Self.* In doing so we'll find even greater strength than whatever we have given away, for God is the Great Replenisher. He has the ability to fill our souls with thousands of loaves when all we have to share with others are a few meager slices. But share we must, for the world's need for nourishment is constant and omnipresent. Yours is the duty to "wake up and do something more!"[33] and as a missionary there is no "someone else" to take care of whatever you leave undone. Whenever the burdens of your life seem difficult to bear, lift your eyes to the world around you, find someone to serve, even in the smallest way, and your own troubles will become lighter and less significant.

Gordon B. Hinckley tells the following story:

> "I recall visiting a college campus where I heard the usual, commonplace complaining of youth: complaints about the pressures of school—as if it were a burden rather than an opportunity to partake of the knowledge of the earth—complaints about housing and about food . . . .

I counseled those youth that if the pressures of school were too heavy, if they felt to complain about their housing and their food, then I could suggest a cure for their problems. I suggested that they lay their books aside for a few hours, leave their rooms, and go visit someone who is old and lonely, or someone sick and discouraged. By and large, I have come to see that if we complain about life, it is because we are thinking only of ourselves.

For many years there was a sign on the wall of a shoe repair shop I patronized. It read, "I complained because I had no shoes until I saw a man who had no feet." The most effective medicine for the sickness of self-pity is to lose ourselves in the service of others."[34]

Without exception, the missionaries we met who were happiest were those who worked hardest. They were willing to let go of their past so God could magnify their present and set them up for a glorious new future. The more you give it all up to God and focus on helping those around you, the more you'll come to understand the old proverb that states, "The mission is your chance to forget your *old* self and become your *true* self."

Ezra Taft Benson taught,

I have often said one of the greatest secrets of missionary work is work! If a missionary works, he will get the Spirit; if he gets the Spirit, he will teach by the Spirit; and if he teaches by the Spirit, he will touch the hearts of the people and he will be happy. There will be no homesickness, no worrying about families, for all time and talents and interests are centered on the work of the ministry. Work, work, work—there is no satisfactory substitute, especially in missionary work.[35]

By choosing faithful obedience and consecrating your whole heart, might, mind, and strength while in the mission field, you will unlock the great blessings God has in store for you. In 1 Corinthians 2:9 it says, "Eye hath not seen, nor ear heard, neither have entered into the heart of man, the things which God hath prepared for them that love him."

Do you hear that promise? We cannot even *imagine* the

The mission is your chance to forget your *old* self and become your *true* self.

blessings God has in store for us; they are literally beyond our comprehension. And how do we show our love for Him exactly? Well, He's not here on the earth with us, but His other children are. What service and love we give them is reflected as if it were given directly to Him (see Mosiah 2:17).

God makes no apologies for inviting you to make huge sacrifices. He wants your *all*. But He promises to give back so much more than anything we've given up. The dividends will far outweigh whatever investment we place in His hands, so trust Him to be good on His promises. As the saying goes, "You can't reach for anything new if your hands are still full of yesterday's junk."

I can't pinpoint the exact moment I got over the feeling of being "Dear John'd,"—that heartache did take quite a bit of time to heal. Nor can I list a specific blessing that was directly connected to letting her go and focusing more deeply on the work of the mission. But I *can* testify of the personal transformation I experienced over the remaining eighteen months, and I know that such a change wouldn't have been possible had I kept a part of my mind and heart focused on her. The Elder Bernards who walked off the plane and greeted his parents at the end of the mission was totally new and different from whoever had left them two years prior.

The best thing I ever did as a missionary was to **forget myself and go to work**.

I promise you that the time you spend in the mission field, if those years are spent in dedicated service, will yield a greater return on investment than any other two years of your lives.

—Gordon B. Hinckley[36]

Persecution has not stopped the progress of truth, but has only added fuel to the flame. It has spread with increasing rapidity. Proud of the cause which they have espoused and conscious of our innocence and of the truth of their system, amidst calumny and reproach, have the elders of this Church gone forth and planted the gospel in almost every state in the Union. It has penetrated our cities; it has spread over our villages and has caused thousands of our intelligent, noble, and patriotic citizens to obey its divine mandates and be governed by its sacred truths. It has also spread into England, Ireland, Scotland, and Wales, where, in the year 1840, a few of our missionaries were sent, and over five thousand joined the Standard of Truth; there are numbers now joining in every land.

Our missionaries are going forth to different nations, and in Germany, Palestine, New Holland, Australia, the East Indies, and other places, the Standard of Truth has been erected; no unhallowed hand can stop the work from progressing; persecutions may rage, mobs may combine, armies may assemble, calumny may defame, but the truth of God will go forth boldly, nobly, and independent, till it has penetrated every continent, visited every clime, swept every country, and sounded in every ear; till the purposes of God shall be accomplished, and the Great Jehovah shall say the work is done.

–Joseph Smith Jr.[37]

CONCLUSION

NGOTATSO:
Now Go Out There and Teach Someone

"On that important day, I have a feeling the question will not be
so much 'What office did you hold?' The real question will be,
'Did you serve me with all your heart, might, mind, and strength?'
God bless us that we may serve so that we will never have
any serious regrets, that we will know we have been
magnified even beyond our own natural talents."

–Ezra Taft Benson[38]

THE BEST MISSION IN THE WORLD

A young man sat quivering with excitement as he waited for his family
to quiet down around him. They were huddled close together in
their family room, watching him as he opened his mission call. The
siblings were chattering and laughing about where they thought he
would go, his mom and dad beaming proudly as they watched him
slowly tear open the large white envelope. He had overcome many
personal struggles in his journey to preparing for a mission and this
moment was especially triumphant. Someone yelled out a bet as to
where he thought he'd be going. South America, like his dad and so
many other kids in his ward? Or Europe like one of his older brothers?
Possibly one of the countries in Asia with newer missionary presence?

The young man finally removed the stack of papers from the
envelope and started reading out loud. The crowd hushed and held
their breath as he announced his location.

A stateside mission in the United States. He was going to Nebraska.

Oh man, I thought, watching it all unfold. *I hope he isn't disappointed . . .*

He sat there for just a moment, smiling and quietly looking at the paper.

"This is *great!*" he finally yelled, as he jumped up and hugged us, laughing. He was excited and thrilled and wasn't let down in the least.

I was so glad to see that he wasn't discouraged with his call. I'd known him a long time and seen how much he'd grown, and knew that he'd make a fantastic missionary.

After all, he was my brother. (Like, literally—he's one of my younger brothers.)

I was thrilled that *he* was thrilled with his mission call and that he wasn't comparing his work or mission to anyone else's. He was firm in the knowledge that God knew him personally and had chosen him to go to that specific area. He knew there were people in Nebraska that only *he* could teach, and that his entire life, both the good and bad that he had experienced, was now part of his preparation and would be invaluably useful as he taught God's children there.

As the years passed and he wrote letters home to his family, his stories and experiences confirmed the fact that he was sent exactly where he needed to go. He didn't need to compare his mission to mine and he didn't need to go to a far-off exotic location in order to be a successful servant. All he needed to do was to stand up and proclaim, "Here am I," when the Lord called him to work.

He believed in the age-old truism: the best mission in the world is the one you have been called to.

Wherever you have been called to go, have faith that God has called you to the right place, at the right time, because He wants you to do something amazing with your life. After all, it's not your mission you are serving—it's His.

The best mission in the world is the one you have been called to.

NGOTATSO

My dad had a funny way of writing letters to his boys on missions. He would use single-page, prepaid international Airmail letters from the post office: it's basically a sheet of paper with a stamp printed on it, and it needs no envelope. You just write on the paper, fold it up, tape it shut, and drop it in a mailbox and it would be mailed anywhere in the world for a flat fee. Since he only had that one sheet of paper to write on, he'd cover every possible square inch with his advice, his counsel, and news from home. At the end of his letters he'd use shorthand for common phrases, and his personal favorite was an acronym of his own creation: **NGOTATSO**.

It was last piece of advice he always gave a missionary—"**Now go out there and teach someone**."

He knew if we were to be successful, we would need to keep moving, keep learning, and keep teaching.

Keep Moving

Most of the time you won't have your own Liahona or pillar of smoke leading you in the wilderness, telling you which way to go. You will be faced with many decisions to make and paths to choose from with seemingly no divine guidance whatsoever. Sometimes we'd see missionaries that would insist on praying for direction as to whether they should turn left or right when out visiting, or they would stop in front of every house and pray for inspiration as to whether or not they should stop and talk. Occasionally they would feel promptings one way or the other, but most of the time they were left to their own choices. When one missionary felt discouraged at this apparent lack of divine guidance, he was reminded that God will not "command in all things," and the entire purpose of this life is for us to learn correct principles and then go forth with our own agency, make our own choices, and roll with whatever the consequences may be. So don't let fear of failure or lack of direction keep you from moving forward. Make the best decision you can with whatever information you have, and let come what may. God will chime in with counsel and direction only when He deems that you really, really need it.

Dallin H. Oaks once gave this counsel to a group of new mission presidents: "In my study of the scriptures I have noted that most revelation to the children of God comes when they are on the move, not when they are sitting back in their habitations waiting for the Lord to tell them the first step to take."[39]

Keep Learning

A quote frequently attributed to Albert Einstein says, "Information is not knowledge. The only source of knowledge is experience."

Put another way, you get what you give, you give what you know, you know what you want to learn. Your mission is a fabulous chance to learn and grow, and you'll gain as much knowledgeable experience as you are willing to receive.

The mission field is unique in its ability to present a constant stream of life lessons and experiences that you wouldn't be able to find anywhere else. Be sure to set aside time for introspection, reflection, and pondering on what you've gone through. Study your experiences from different angles, chew them over, and list what you've learned from them. One missionary I knew had an entry in his journal where he listed every companion he worked with or area in which he served, with a summary sentence of what he learned from that person or place. He may not have remembered every detail of his day-to-day work, but he made sure to record the lessons he gained and embed those truths deep in his heart.

Keep Teaching

My first companion in Lifou was an incredibly gifted teacher. His quiet confidence in the gospel, his obedience to the rules, and his dependency on the Spirit to magnify his talents all combined to produce a gift of fellowshipping and teaching that wrought many miracles. Part of his skill was his ability to naturally talk to and teach anyone he encountered. I noticed this in particular as we drove him to the airport on his last day on the mission. We had to stop for gas, and I found him chatting with the gas station attendant, introducing himself as a missionary and befriending the man. Even as he was departing from the island, he made sure that every last minute was spent in the service of God. Everyone he met was a chance to teach. He lived the great missionary commission penned by Bruce R. McConkie while he was a mission president:

"I am called of God. My authority is above that of the kings of the earth. By revelation I have been selected as a personal representative of the Lord Jesus Christ. He is my Master and He has chosen me to represent Him. To stand in His place, to say and do what He himself would say and do if He personally were ministering to the very people to whom He has sent me. My voice is His voice, and my acts are His acts; my words are His words and my doctrine is His doctrine. My commission is to do what He wants done. To say what He wants said. To be a living modern witness in word and deed of the divinity of His great and marvelous latter-day work. How great is my calling."[40]

FAITH AND A LIFE JACKET

A young friend shared this sobering experience from the last few days of his mission. He said that the night before he went home, the group of returning missionaries held a testimony meeting with the mission president. They all gave pretty standard statements, except for one young man. This missionary stood up in front of the group and started sobbing. He said he would always regret the last seven and a half months of his mission, because he had spent most of his time sleeping, cooking, eating, playing piano, and visiting members, with almost zero actual missionary work.

He talked about how some of his junior companions would try to get him to work, but they would always eventually end up just doing language study while he wasted his time. Other companions were happy to be paired with him for a time, thinking they'd have that transfer period "off duty" and would just do whatever he did.

When his final transfer came, he said he decided to work hard for the last couple of weeks and convince himself that he'd done his best. But it didn't work. He still felt panic and shame when he looked back at what he'd done (or hadn't done) for that area and branch in the nine months he was there. He'd had zero baptisms, zero reactivations, and only actually taught a few dozen lessons, most of which were just member visits.

However, he did end on a positive note, saying that he had learned his lesson and would never idle away his time again. As the young man said, "The point is: don't be him."

There is no way to "cram" missionary work into a short amount of time. There is no rewind button, no do-overs, and you don't get to respawn at the end. You get one shot, and that's it. You alone have the power to decide whether your final day as a missionary will be filled with regret and remorse, or quiet, triumphant satisfaction in the knowledge that you had wrung yourself out in the service of God.

I hope these 7 Truths for your Eternal Mission have been helpful to you. I believe that as you learn of them and apply them in your life (whether as a pre-missionary, a missionary currently serving, or a member having moved on to the next chapter of your life), they'll continually guide you and help you on to that stage of "Emotional Self-Reliance" we talked about way back at the beginning. I hope these truths become stepping-stones to greater light and knowledge, and that you learn even *more* truths along the way. There's so much out there to learn!

Your mission experience is going to be a wonderfully difficult, unique, challenging experience, custom-tailored just for you. It won't be easy, but it's *so* worth it. Sometimes God will heed your cries and calm the storms of your missionary trials. And other times you'll have to ride it out, with no miracles to be found besides those of your own making. That's the beautiful duality of our relationship with God, and the reality of being a missionary in these latter days. It's the whole "pray as if everything depended on God, work as if everything depended on you" principle. It's "Christ's grace is strong enough to save, *after* everything we can do."

It won't be easy, but it's *so* worth it.

When we are asked to walk on the water, maybe we really *do* need both faith and a life jacket. I hope you find both.

❧

May you have a wonderful mission, and may you always go to bed utterly exhausted.

You've had 19 years to prepare for it.

You have 2 years to work on it.

You'll have an eternity to reflect on it.

Now go out there and teach someone.

You have so little time.

ENDNOTES

1. Ezra Taft Benson, *The Teachings of Ezra Taft Benson* (Salt Lake City: Bookcraft, 1988), 192.
2. Scott Krippayne "Sometimes He Calms The Storm."
3. Joseph Smith, *History of The Church of Jesus Christ of Latter-day Saints*. Edited by B. H. Roberts. 2nd ed. rev., 7 vols. (Salt Lake City: The Church of Jesus Christ of Latter-day Saints, 1932–51), 5:401.
4. Thomas S. Monson, *Pathways to Perfection: Discourses of Thomas S. Monson* (Salt Lake City: Deseret Book, 1984).
5. Gordan B. Hinckley, "To the Women of the Church," *Ensign*, November 2003.
6. Louisa May Alcott, *Little Women* (New York: Random House, 2007).
7. Dieter F. Uchtdorf, "Your Happily Ever After," *Ensign*, May 2010.
8. *Journal of Discourses* (London: Latter-day Saints' Book Depot, 1854–86) vol. 25, 209.
9. The ceremonial greeting customs with their chiefs.
10. As cited in Orson F. Whitney, *Life of Heber C. Kimball* (Salt Lake City: Bookcraft, 1967), 132.
11. James E. Faust, "What I Want My Son to Know before He Leaves on His Mission," *Ensign*, May 1996, 42.
12. Bob Moorehead, *Words Aptly Spoken* (Overlake Christian Bookstore, 1995).
13. A Melanesian musical style, similar to reggae.

14. Ezra Taft Benson, as quoted in Donald L. Staheli, "Obedience—Life's Great Challenge," *Ensign*, May 1998, 82.

15. *Preach My Gospel: A Guide to Missionary Service* (2004), 155–74.

16. LDS Church News Release, October 6 2012; emphasis added.

17. Neal A. Maxwell, *Even As I Am* (Salt Lake City: Deseret Book, 1982), 93.

18. *Documentary History of the Church*, 5:517.

19. Jeffrey R. Holland, "The Tongue of Angels," *Ensign*, May 2007.

20. In Conference Report, April 1917, 43

21. *History of the Church*, 4:227

22. Joseph Smith, *Teachings of the Prophet Joseph Smith* (Salt Lake City: Deseret Book, 1976), 313.

23. Steven R. Covey, *The Seven Habits of Highly Effective People* (New York: Simon & Schuster, 1989), 219–20.

24. David A. Bednar, "Becoming a Missionary," *Ensign*, November 2005, 45; emphasis added.

25. See *Teachings of Presidents of the Church—Joseph Smith* (Salt Lake City: The Church of Jesus Christ of Latter-day Saints, 2011), 36–44.

26. Gordon B. Hinckley, "Find the Lambs, Feed the Sheep," *Ensign*, May 1999, 106.

27. *Preach My Gospel*, 11.

28. Marvin J. Ashton, "The Measure of Our Hearts," *Ensign*, November 1988.

29. Ezra Taft Benson, "Jesus Christ—Gifts and Expectations," *Ensign*, December 1988.

30. Gordon B. Hinckley, "Discover Yourself," *Millennial Star* 95, no. 36 (1933): 606.

31. *Scrapbook of Mormon Literature*, vol. 2, 173.

32. Gordon B. Hinckley, "Taking the Gospel to Britain: A Declaration of Vision, Faith, Courage, and Truth," *Ensign*, July 1987, 7.

33. "Have I Done Any Good?" *Hymns*, no. 223.

34. Gordon B. Hinckley, "'Whosoever Will Save His Life,'" *Ensign*, August 1982, 5.

35. Benson, *Teachings of Ezra Taft Benson*, 200.

36. Gordon B. Hinckley, "Of Missions, Temples, and Stewardship," *Ensign*, November 1995, 52.

37. "The Wentworth Letter," March 1, 1842.

38. Ezra Taft Benson, "Keys to Successful Member-Missionary Work," *Ensign*, September 1990.
39. New Mission Presidents Address, June 27, 2001.
40. Mission president address, Australian Mission, 1961–64.

SPECIAL THANKS

To El Stone for the beautiful photography and being the head cheerleader, Brad Wilcox for believing in me, Brian and Laura Hales, Jean Tefan, Kevin Ball, Nate Phillips, Jon Hilton, Tomi Ann Hill, the Bernards Clan, and the wonderful team at Cedar Fort publishing,

and most of all my sweet wife, Megan.

ABOUT THE AUTHOR

Ben grew up in a big Mormon family in a small farming town in the heart of Utah County where he and his eight brothers and sisters were raised on a steady diet of Nintendo, Transformers, Dungeons & Dragons, and Star Wars. He geeks out on all that plus everything marching band, Marvel, and Tolkien. (His autographed edition of *The Lord of the Rings* is pretty much the coolest.)

He loves teaching youth the gospel, whether it be in seminary, Sunday School, youth conferences, or (his favorite) Especially for Youth. He served a mission, but you'll have to read the book to see where. (He only mentions it, like, what, 100 times?)

After completing his master's in information systems management from Brigham Young University, he was lucky enough to both marry his college sweetheart and land a job where shorts and a T-shirt are acceptable attire and his action figures can be displayed with pride. He's a project manager and systems analyst for a certain fruity computer company and loves to tinker around with app design and UX projects on the side.

At home, he has a pretty sweet board game collection and is secretly envious of his kids' Lego toys. He lives in northern California where he loves to run trails with his wife and make plans for building his own hobbit hole in the backyard. He's hoping this won't be his only book.